PANENTHEISM
A BEGINNER'S GUIDE

EXPLORING THE DIVINE IN ALL THINGS

MATTHEW ADAMS

For Mom and Dad

The divine is not far away, but near; it is not separate from the world, but deeply woven into its fabric. To see the world as infused with the sacred is to recognize the presence of the divine in all things.

— ANONYMOUS

CONTENTS

INTRODUCTION

DEFINITION OF PANENTHEISM

Panentheism is a theological concept that posits God is both immanent and transcendent. This means God exists within the universe but also extends beyond it. Panentheism bridges the gap, unlike traditional theism, which sees God as entirely separate from the world. It provides a view where the divine permeates all aspects of life and the universe. This unique perspective offers a more interconnected understanding of spirituality and existence.

The term "panentheism" combines the Greek words "pan" (all), "en" (in), and "theos" (God). It literally translates to "all-in-God". This concept suggests that everything is within God, but God is also greater than everything. This idea can be challenging to grasp initially because it blurs the lines between the divine and the mundane. Yet, this very charac-teristic is what makes panentheism appealing to many spiri-tual seekers.

Panentheism is not confined to any single religion or philosophy. It can be found in various forms across different traditions and cultures. Each tradition may have its unique interpretation, but the core idea remains consistent. This universality highlights the flexibility and adaptability of panentheism as a spiritual framework.

Practically, panentheism invites individuals to see the sacred in everyday life. It encourages a holistic view where the divine is present in nature, relationships, and personal experiences. This perspective can lead to a deeper sense of connection and reverence for the world around us.

Panentheism also offers a framework for understanding the dynamic relationship between the divine and the world. It suggests that God is not a distant, uninvolved deity but an active, integral part of the universe. This relationship is not static but continually evolving, reflecting the ongoing interaction between the divine and creation.

ROOTS IN ANCIENT PHILOSOPHIES

The roots of panentheism can be traced back to ancient philosophies and spiritual traditions. In ancient Greece, philosophers like Plato and Aristotle explored ideas that resonated with panentheistic thought. Plato's concept of the World Soul and Aristotle's notion of the Prime Mover both suggest a divine presence that is intimately connected to the world yet surpasses it.

In Eastern traditions, panentheistic ideas can be found in Hinduism and Buddhism. The Upanishads, ancient Hindu scriptures, describe Brahman as the ultimate reality that permeates everything. Similarly, Buddhist teachings often speak of the interconnectedness of all life, a concept that aligns with panentheistic views. These ancient texts provide a rich foundation for understanding how different cultures have approached the idea of a divine presence within the world.

The influence of panentheistic ideas is also evident in indigenous spiritual practices. Many indigenous cultures have a deep reverence for nature and see the divine in the natural world. This perspective aligns closely with panentheism, emphasizing the sacredness of all life and the interconnectedness of all beings.

In the Middle Ages, mystics and theologians further developed panentheistic thought. Figures like Meister Eckhart and Hildegard of Bingen wrote about their experiences of God's presence in the world. Their writings reflect a deep sense of unity with the divine, which is characteristic of panentheistic spirituality.

These historical roots demonstrate that panentheism is not a new or isolated concept. It has been a part of human spiritual exploration for millennia, evolving and adapting to different cultural contexts. Understanding these roots helps to appreciate the depth and diversity of panentheistic thought.

CORE PRINCIPLES

At its core, panentheism is built on several key principles that define its unique spiritual approach. First and foremost is the belief in God's immanence and transcendence. This means that God is present within all aspects of the universe while also existing beyond it. This dual nature of the divine is a fundamental aspect of panentheistic thought.

Another core principle is the interconnectedness of all life. Panentheism posits that everything in the universe is connected through the divine presence. This interconnectedness fosters a sense of unity and oneness, encouraging a holistic view of life and spirituality. It suggests that all beings are part of a larger, divine whole.

The principle of dynamic interaction is also central to panentheism. Unlike static views of God, panentheism sees the divine as actively involved in the world. This ongoing interaction between God and creation reflects the evolving nature of the universe and the divine presence within it. It emphasizes that the relationship between God and the world is not fixed but continually developing.

Panentheism also highlights the sacredness of the material world. In this view, the physical universe is not separate from the divine but an expression of it. This principle encourages a reverence for nature and a recognition of the divine in everyday life. It challenges the dualistic separation of the sacred and the profane.

Ethical responsibility is another important principle. Panentheism suggests that because the divine is present in all things, how we treat the world and each other matters. This perspective encourages a sense of stewardship and care for the environment and all living beings. It fosters a moral framework based on the interconnectedness and sacredness of life.

PANENTHEISM VS. PANTHEISM

While panentheism and pantheism may seem similar, they differ in significant ways. Pantheism asserts that God and the universe are identical, meaning everything collectively is God. On the other hand, Panentheism maintains that while God is in everything, God also transcends the universe. This distinction is crucial for understanding the nuanced view of the divine in panentheism.

Pantheism views the universe as divine without distinguishing between the Creator and creation. This perspective can lead to a more impersonal view of the divine, where God is seen as the sum total of all that exists. In contrast, panentheism maintains a personal aspect of the divine, suggesting that while God is within everything, God also has an existence beyond the material world.

The differences between these two views also influence their theological implications. Pantheism often emphasizes the unity and sameness of all things, promoting a view that everything is equally divine. Panentheism, however, allows for a more complex relationship between the divine and the world, recognizing the unity and the distinction between God and creation.

In practical terms, these differences can affect how individuals experience and relate to the divine. Pantheism might encourage a more detached, contemplative approach, focusing on the oneness of all existence. On the other hand, Panentheism fosters a sense of active engagement with the world, seeing every action and relationship as a reflection of the divine presence.

Understanding these distinctions helps clarify panentheism's unique contributions to spiritual thought. It offers a more flexible and dynamic framework for understanding the divine, one that acknowledges both God's immanence and transcendence. This nuanced view can provide a richer and more inclusive spiritual experience.

ROLE OF GOD IN PANENTHEISM

In panentheism, God's role is multifaceted and dynamic. God is seen as the source of all creation, imbuing the universe with divine presence while also existing beyond it. This dual role highlights the complexity and depth of the divine in panentheistic thought. It suggests a God who is intimately involved with the world and transcendent beyond the confines of the physical universe.

God's immanence in panentheism means that the divine presence permeates every aspect of the universe. This presence is not limited to sacred spaces or religious practices but is found in all aspects of life. It encourages a view of the world where everything is infused with divine significance, from the smallest particle to the vast cosmos.

The transcendence of God in panentheism emphasizes that while God is present within the universe, God also exists beyond it. This aspect of the divine suggests a reality that surpasses human understanding and the material world. It invites a sense of awe and mystery, recognizing that the divine is greater than the sum of its parts.

In panentheistic thought, God is also seen as the sustainer and nurturer of the universe. This role suggests an ongoing, dynamic relationship between the divine and creation. It implies that God is actively involved in the world, guiding and supporting the unfolding of the universe. This perspective can provide a sense of purpose and direction in life.

The role of God in panentheism also includes a personal aspect. While the divine presence is universal, it is also accessible to individuals. Panentheism suggests that personal experiences of the divine reflect the broader, interconnected reality of God. This personal connection can deepen one's spiritual practice and understanding.

PANENTHEISM IN VARIOUS RELIGIONS

Panentheism is a concept that transcends cultural and religious boundaries. It can be found in various forms across different religious traditions. In Hinduism, for example, the idea of Brahman as the ultimate reality that permeates everything aligns closely with panentheistic thought. The Upanishads and other sacred texts describe a divine presence that is both immanent and transcendent.

In Christianity, panentheistic ideas can be seen in the writings of mystics like Meister Eckhart and Julian of Norwich. These mystics spoke of experiencing God's presence in all things, reflecting a panentheistic view. The Christian concept of the Holy Spirit also resonates with panentheistic ideas, suggesting a divine presence that is active and immanent in the world.

Islamic mysticism, or Sufism, also incorporates panentheistic elements. Sufi poets and scholars often describe the divine as present in all aspects of life. Rumi's writings, for example, are filled with references to a God who is both within and beyond the world. This perspective emphasizes the interconnectedness of all creation and the divine.

In Buddhism, particularly in Mahayana and Zen traditions, the concept of emptiness and the interdependence of all things can be seen as reflecting panentheistic ideas. These teachings suggest a reality where all things are connected through a fundamental, underlying truth. This view aligns with the panentheistic idea of a divine presence that permeates everything.

Indigenous spiritual practices around the world also reflect panentheistic principles. Many indigenous cultures deeply revere nature and see the divine in the natural world. This perspective emphasizes the sacredness of all life and the interconnectedness of all beings. It highlights the universality and adaptability of panentheistic thought.

MODERN PERSPECTIVES

In modern times, panentheism has evolved and adapted to contemporary spiritual and philosophical thought. It remains a relevant and influential framework for understanding the divine and the universe. Modern theologians and philosophers have expanded on traditional panentheistic ideas, exploring their implications for science, ecology, and ethics.

One area where panentheism has gained traction is in the dialogue between science and religion. The interconnectedness and dynamic nature of the universe suggested by panentheism resonate with scientific discoveries in fields like quantum physics and cosmology, leading to a renewed interest in panentheistic ideas among scholars and thinkers.

Environmentalism is another area where panentheism has found a modern application. Recognizing the divine presence in nature aligns with ecological concerns and the need for environmental stewardship. Panentheism provides a spiritual and ethical foundation for caring for the planet, emphasizing the interconnectedness of all life.

In contemporary spirituality, panentheism offers a flexible and inclusive framework. It appeals to those who seek a deeper connection with the divine that is not confined to traditional religious structures. This perspective encourages a holistic and experiential approach to spirituality, recognizing the sacred in everyday life.

Modern panentheism also engages with ethical and social issues. The interconnectedness of all beings suggested by panentheistic thought implies a moral responsibility to care for each other and the world. This perspective can inform approaches to social justice, human rights, and global interconnectivity, offering a spiritual foundation for addressing contemporary challenges.

Modern perspectives on panentheism demonstrate its continued relevance and adaptability. It provides a rich and nuanced framework for exploring the divine, the universe, and our place within it. This dynamic and evolving tradition inspires and guides spiritual seekers and thinkers in the contemporary world.

HISTORICAL ORIGINS

EARLY PHILOSOPHICAL ROOTS

The roots of panentheism stretch back to ancient Greece. Early philosophers like Plato and Aristotle explored ideas about the divine that resonate with panentheism. Plato's concept of the World Soul, an animating force present in all things, suggests a divine presence intertwined with the universe. Aristotle's notion of the Prime Mover, a perfect and eternal source of all motion, also hints at a transcendent yet immanent divine force.

These philosophical ideas were revolutionary for their time. They challenged the traditional views of gods as separate beings who lived on Mount Olympus or other distant realms. Instead, they suggested that the divine was an integral part of the cosmos itself. This shift in thinking laid the groundwork for later theological developments.

Ancient Greek philosophy wasn't just about abstract thought. It also had practical implications for how people understood their place in the world. By suggesting that the divine was present in everything, these early philosophers encouraged a more holistic view of existence. This perspective fostered a sense of unity and interconnectedness that would become central to panentheistic thought.

These early ideas didn't stay confined to Greece. They spread throughout the Mediterranean and beyond, influencing other cultures and philosophical traditions. As they traveled, they were adapted and integrated into new contexts, blending with local beliefs and practices. This cross-pollination of ideas enriched the philosophical landscape and laid the foundation for the diverse expressions of panentheism we see today.

The early philosophical roots of panentheism show how ancient thinkers grappled with profound questions about the nature of the divine and the universe. Their insights continue to inspire and inform contemporary discussions about spirituality and the nature of existence.

INFLUENCE OF ANCIENT CULTURES

The influence of panentheistic ideas wasn't limited to ancient Greece. Many ancient cultures had their own versions of these concepts. In India, the Upanishads, sacred texts of Hinduism, describe Brahman as the ultimate reality that pervades everything. This idea closely aligns with panentheism, suggesting an immanent and transcendent divine presence.

In China, Taoist philosophy also reflects panentheistic themes. The Tao, or the Way, is seen as the underlying principle that flows through all life. It is both within and beyond the world, guiding the natural order and the rhythms of the universe. This perspective emphasizes harmony and balance, key aspects of panentheistic thought.

Indigenous cultures around the world also hold panentheistic beliefs. Many Native American traditions, for example, see the Great Spirit as present in all aspects of nature. This belief fosters a deep respect for the environment and a recognition of the interconnectedness of all life. It reflects a worldview where the divine is not separate from the world but embedded within it.

These ancient cultures contributed to a rich tapestry of panentheistic thought. By recognizing the divine in the world around them, they cultivated a sense of reverence and connection to the natural world. This perspective influenced their spiritual practices, rituals, and ways of life, creating a holistic approach to existence.

The influence of these ancient cultures on panentheism highlights the universality of this concept. It shows how different peoples, separated by time and geography, have arrived at similar understandings of the divine. This universality underscores the enduring appeal of panentheistic ideas and their relevance to human spirituality.

DEVELOPMENT THROUGH THE MIDDLE AGES

During the Middle Ages, panentheistic ideas continued to evolve and find expression in various religious and philosophical contexts. Christian mystics like Meister Eckhart and Hildegard of Bingen wrote about their experiences of God's presence in the world. They described a divine force that was both within and beyond creation, reflecting a panentheistic view.

Islamic mysticism, or Sufism, also embraced panentheistic ideas. Sufi poets and scholars spoke of the divine as present in all aspects of life. Rumi's writings, for example, are filled with references to a God who is both within and beyond the world. This perspective emphasizes the interconnectedness of all creation and the divine.

Jewish mysticism, particularly the Kabbalah, also reflects panentheistic themes. The Kabbalistic concept of Ein Sof, the infinite and unknowable aspect of God, suggests a divine presence that permeates all things. This idea aligns closely with panentheism, highlighting the unity and diversity of the divine.

During this period, panentheistic ideas were often expressed through mystical experiences and spiritual practices. Mystics from various traditions described profound encounters with the divine, where they felt a deep sense of unity with all of creation. These experiences reinforced the idea of an immanent and transcendent God, central to panentheistic thought.

The development of panentheism during the Middle Ages shows how these ideas continued to evolve and find new expressions. It highlights the rich diversity of panentheistic thought and its ability to adapt to different cultural and religious contexts. This period laid the groundwork for further developments in the Renaissance and beyond.

RENAISSANCE AND ENLIGHTENMENT CONTRIBUTIONS

The Renaissance and Enlightenment periods brought new energy and insights to panentheistic thought. The Renaissance, with its emphasis on humanism and the rediscovery of classical texts, revived interest in ancient philosophical ideas. Thinkers like Giordano Bruno and Nicholas of Cusa explored panentheistic concepts, suggesting that God was present in the infinite universe and all its parts.

Bruno's vision of an infinite universe filled with countless worlds challenged the traditional, geocentric view of the cosmos. He proposed that the divine was not confined to a single place but permeated the entire universe. This radical idea expanded the scope of panentheistic thought, emphasizing the vastness and immanence of the divine.

During the Enlightenment, philosophers like Spinoza offered new interpretations of panentheistic ideas. Spinoza's concept of God as the underlying substance of everything suggested a divine presence that was both immanent and transcendent. His work laid the groundwork for modern pantheism and panentheism, blending rationalism with spiritual insight.

The Enlightenment also saw the rise of scientific inquiry, which influenced panentheistic thought. The discoveries of the natural world, from the vastness of space to the complexity of life, inspired new ways of understanding the divine. Panentheism provided a framework for integrating these scientific insights with a spiritual perspective, emphasizing the interconnectedness of all things.

5

These contributions from the Renaissance and Enlightenment periods highlight the dynamic and evolving nature of panentheism. They show how new ideas and discoveries can enrich and expand our understanding of the divine. This period of intellectual and cultural flourishing laid the foundation for contemporary panentheistic thought.

KEY HISTORICAL FIGURES

Several key historical figures have played pivotal roles in the development of panentheism. In the early Christian era, figures like Origen and Gregory of Nyssa explored ideas about the divine that aligned with panentheistic thought. Their writings emphasized God's immanence and transcendence, suggesting a divine presence within creation.

In the Middle Ages, mystics like Meister Eckhart and Hildegard of Bingen brought panentheistic ideas to life through their profound spiritual experiences. Eckhart's sermons and writings described a God who is both within and beyond the world, while Hildegard's visionary works conveyed a deep sense of the divine presence in nature.

During the Renaissance, thinkers like Giordano Bruno and Nicholas of Cusa pushed the boundaries of panentheistic thought. Bruno's vision of an infinite universe filled with divine presence challenged conventional views, while Cusa's mystical theology emphasized the unity of God and creation.

In the Enlightenment, philosophers like Spinoza offered new interpretations of panentheistic ideas. Spinoza's work blended rationalism with spiritual insight, suggesting a God who is the substance and essence of all things. His ideas have had a lasting impact on modern panentheism.

These historical figures have contributed to the rich tapestry of panentheistic thought. Their insights and experiences have shaped the development of this concept, highlighting its depth and diversity. By exploring their contributions, we gain a deeper understanding of panentheism's enduring appeal and relevance.

EVOLUTION OVER CENTURIES

Panentheism has evolved significantly over the centuries, adapting to new cultural, intellectual, and spiritual contexts. In ancient times, it emerged as a philosophical response to questions about the nature of the divine and the universe. As these ideas spread and interacted with different traditions, they evolved into diverse expressions of panentheistic thought.

During the Middle Ages, panentheism was expressed in mystical experiences and theological writings. Mystics from various traditions described encounters with the divine that emphasized both immanence and transcendence. These experiences reinforced the idea of a God intimately connected to the world yet beyond it.

The Renaissance and Enlightenment periods brought new energy and insights to panentheism. The rediscovery of classical texts and the rise of scientific inquiry expanded the scope of panentheistic thought. Thinkers like Giordano Bruno and Spinoza offered new interpretations, integrating ancient ideas with contemporary discoveries.

Panentheism continues to evolve in modern times, influenced by developments in science, ecology, and spirituality. Scientific discoveries in fields like quantum physics and cosmology emphasize the interconnectedness of all life, which resonates with panentheistic ideas. This has renewed interest in panentheism among scholars and spiritual seekers.

The evolution of panentheism over the centuries shows its adaptability and relevance. It highlights how this concept has grown and changed in response to new insights and challenges. By tracing its development, we can appreciate the depth and diversity of panentheistic thought and its continuing impact on contemporary spirituality.

IMPACT ON CONTEMPORARY THOUGHT

Panentheism has significantly impacted contemporary thought, influencing various fields, including theology, philosophy, science, and environmentalism. Its emphasis on the interconnectedness of all life resonates with modern scientific discoveries, such as the interconnectedness of ecosystems and the universe's complexity.

In theology, panentheism offers a framework for understanding the divine that integrates traditional religious beliefs with contemporary insights. It provides a way to reconcile God's immanence and transcendence, suggesting a dynamic relationship between the divine and the world. This perspective has inspired new theological approaches and spiritual practices.

Philosophically, panentheism challenges dualistic thinking and encourages a more holistic view of existence. It emphasizes the unity and diversity of the divine, suggesting that God is both within and beyond creation. This perspective has influenced contemporary philosophical discussions about the nature of reality and the relationship between mind and matter.

Panentheism offers a framework for integrating scientific discoveries with spiritual insights. Fields like quantum physics and cosmology emphasize the interconnectedness of all things, which aligns with panentheistic ideas. This integration provides a richer understanding of the universe and our place within it.

Environmentalism has also been influenced by panentheistic thought. Recognizing the divine presence in nature encourages a sense of reverence and responsibility for the environment. Panentheism provides a spiritual and ethical foundation for environmental stewardship, emphasizing the interconnectedness and sacredness of all life.

Panentheism's impact on contemporary thought highlights its relevance and adaptability. It shows how this concept continues to inspire and inform discussions about the nature of the divine, the universe, and our place within it. Panentheism offers a rich and nuanced framework for exploring these profound questions.

KEY CONCEPTS AND PRINCIPLES

IMMANENCE AND TRANSCENDENCE

Immanence and transcendence are core ideas in panentheism. Immanence means that God is present in all things. It's the idea that the divine is deeply embedded in the world around us. Everything is infused with God's presence, from the tiniest particles to the vast expanses of space.

Transcendence, on the other hand, means that God is beyond all things. God is not limited by the physical universe. This suggests a divine presence that surpasses our understanding and exists outside time and space constraints. Together, immanence and transcendence create a dynamic view of the divine.

In panentheism, these concepts are not opposites but complementary. They work together to describe a God within and beyond the universe. This view encourages us to see the divine in everyday life while acknowledging a greater mystery we can never fully comprehend.

Immanence makes the divine accessible and relatable. It allows people to feel connected to God through their experiences in the world. Transcendence, meanwhile, invites a sense of awe and wonder, reminding us of the infinite nature of the divine. This balance between immanence and transcendence is what makes panentheism unique.

Understanding immanence and transcendence helps us appreciate the depth of panentheistic thought. It shows how this belief system integrates the divine into all aspects of life while recognizing God's vastness and mystery. This dual perspective enriches our spiritual understanding and experience.

THE NATURE OF GOD

In panentheism, the nature of God is both complex and profound. God is seen as the source of all existence, the creative force behind everything. This divine presence is not static but dynamic, constantly interacting with the world. God is both the creator and sustainer of the universe.

This view of God emphasizes both immanence and transcendence. As an immanent presence, God is intimately involved in the world, present in every moment and every place. This makes the divine accessible and personal, allowing individuals to experience God in their daily lives.

At the same time, God is transcendent, existing beyond the physical universe. This aspect of the divine surpasses human understanding and encompasses all of reality. It suggests a greater mystery that invites awe and reverence. This transcendence adds a layer of depth to our understanding of the divine.

The nature of God in panentheism also includes a relational aspect. God is not a distant, detached being but one that is deeply connected to creation. This relationship is dynamic and evolving, reflecting the ongoing interaction between the divine and the world. It suggests that God is actively engaged in the unfolding of the universe.

The nature of God in panentheism is rich and multifaceted. It challenges simple definitions and invites a deeper exploration of the divine. By understanding this complexity, we gain a more profound appreciation of the interconnectedness of all things and the divine presence that permeates everything.

THE UNIVERSE AND ITS RELATIONSHIP TO GOD

In panentheism, the universe and its relationship to God are central themes. The universe is seen as a manifestation of the divine, a physical expression of God's presence. This means that everything in the universe is somehow connected to the divine. The stars, planets, and all life forms are part of a larger, interconnected whole.

This relationship is dynamic and evolving. God is not a passive observer but an active participant in the universe. This suggests that the divine presence constantly interacts with and influences the unfolding of the cosmos, highlighting the idea that creation is an ongoing process.

Panentheism also emphasizes the sacredness of the universe. Because the divine is present in everything, every part of the universe holds spiritual significance. This perspective encourages a deep reverence for the natural world and all its inhabitants. It suggests that caring for the environment is a form of spiritual practice.

The relationship between the universe and God also includes the idea of unity and diversity. While everything is connected through the divine, each part of creation is recognized as unique and individual. This balance between unity and diversity enriches our understanding of the universe and its relationship to God.

Understanding the universe in the context of panentheism invites a holistic view of existence. It encourages us to see the divine in all aspects of life and to recognize the interconnectedness of all things. This perspective fosters a sense of wonder and appreciation for the world around us and our place within it.

SPIRITUAL AND MATERIAL WORLDS

Panentheism blurs the line between the spiritual and material worlds. In this view, the material world is not separate from the divine but an expression of it. This means that the physical universe is infused with spiritual significance. Everything we see and experience in the material world reflects the divine presence.

This perspective challenges the traditional dualistic view that separates the sacred and the profane. Instead, it suggests that the divine is present in all aspects of life, from the mundane to the extraordinary. This idea encourages a holistic approach to spirituality, where everyday experiences are seen as opportunities to connect with the divine.

In panentheism, the spiritual and material worlds are interconnected and interdependent. The material world provides a context for spiritual growth and development. Through our experiences in the physical world, we can understand and appreciate the divine presence. This interconnectedness enriches our spiritual practice and understanding.

This view also emphasizes the importance of the material world in our spiritual journey. It suggests that caring for the environment and engaging in ethical behavior are integral to spiritual practice. Recognizing the divine in the material world encourages us to treat all aspects of life with reverence and respect.

Understanding the relationship between the spiritual and material worlds in panentheism invites a deeper appreciation of the divine presence in all things. It encourages a holistic and integrated approach to spirituality, where the sacred is found in the everyday and the divine is present in all aspects of life.

PANENTHEISTIC COSMOLOGY

Panentheistic cosmology offers a unique perspective on the nature and structure of the universe. It suggests that the cosmos is a manifestation of the divine presence, with God permeating every part of it. This view sees the universe as an interconnected whole, where everything is infused with spiritual significance.

In this cosmology, the universe is not static but dynamic and evolving. The divine presence is actively involved in the unfolding of the cosmos, guiding and sustaining its development. This suggests a continuous interaction between the divine and the material world, reflecting the ongoing creation process.

This perspective also emphasizes the universe's unity and diversity. While everything is connected through the divine presence, each part of creation is unique and individual. This balance between unity and diversity enriches our understanding of the cosmos and its relationship to the divine.

Panentheistic cosmology also includes the idea of immanence and transcendence. The divine is present within the universe, imbuing every aspect with spiritual significance. At the same time, God is beyond the physical universe, existing outside time and space constraints. This dual perspective adds depth and complexity to our understanding of the cosmos.

Panentheistic cosmology offers a holistic and integrated view of the universe. It encourages us to see the divine in all aspects of life and recognize all things' interconnectedness. This perspective fosters a sense of wonder and appreciation for the cosmos and our place within it.

THE ROLE OF HUMANITY

In panentheism, humanity has a unique and important role within the cosmos. Humans are seen as part of the interconnected web of life, with a special capacity to recognize and respond to the divine presence. This perspective emphasizes the idea that humans are both physical and spiritual beings, capable of bridging the material and spiritual worlds.

This view suggests that humans have a responsibility to care for the world around them. Because the divine is present in all things, how we treat the environment and other beings matters. This ethical responsibility encourages a sense of stewardship and care for the planet and all its inhabitants.

Humanity's role also includes the pursuit of spiritual growth and development. By recognizing the divine presence in the world and in ourselves, we are encouraged to cultivate a deeper understanding and connection with the divine. This spiritual journey is seen as an integral part of human life, enriching our experiences and relationships.

Panentheism also emphasizes the importance of community and interconnectedness. Humans are not isolated beings but part of a larger, interconnected whole. This perspective encourages a sense of solidarity and compassion, fostering relationships based on mutual respect and understanding.

Understanding the role of humanity in panentheism invites a holistic view of life. It encourages us to see our actions and relationships as part of a larger spiritual context. This perspective fosters a sense of purpose and responsibility, guiding us toward ethical and compassionate living.

ETHICAL IMPLICATIONS

The ethical implications of panentheism are profound and far-reaching. This perspective suggests that because the divine is present in all things, how we treat the world and each other is of utmost importance. It provides a spiritual foundation for ethical behavior, emphasizing the interconnectedness and sacredness of all life.

One key ethical implication is the responsibility to care for the environment. Panentheism encourages a deep reverence for nature, recognizing the divine presence in the natural world. This perspective fosters a sense of stewardship, encouraging sustainable practices and the protection of the planet.

Panentheism also emphasizes the importance of compassion and empathy. Recognizing the divine presence in all beings encourages us to treat others with kindness and respect. This ethical framework promotes social justice, human rights, and the well-being of all individuals.

This perspective also encourages a holistic approach to ethics. It suggests that ethical behavior is not limited to specific actions but encompasses our entire way of life. This holistic view integrates spirituality and ethics, encouraging us to live harmoniously with the divine presence in all things.

Panentheism's ethical implications provide a rich and nuanced framework for living a compassionate and responsible life. By recognizing the interconnectedness and sacredness of all life, we are guided toward ethical behavior that respects and honors the divine presence in the world. This perspective fosters a sense of purpose and responsibility, enriching our spiritual and ethical understanding.

PANENTHEISM IN EASTERN RELIGIONS

HINDUISM AND PANENTHEISM

Hinduism is one of the oldest religions in the world and has many ideas that align with panentheism. Central to Hindu belief is Brahman, the ultimate reality or cosmic spirit. Brahman is seen as the source of all creation, present in every part of the universe, yet also transcending it. This idea fits well with panentheistic thought, where the divine is within and beyond the material world.

In Hinduism, the concept of Atman, or the individual soul, is considered a part of Brahman. This suggests that each person has a divine essence within them, connecting them to the larger cosmic reality. This connection reflects the panentheistic view that the divine permeates all aspects of existence, making everything sacred.

Hindu scriptures like the Upanishads and the Bhagavad Gita explore these ideas in depth. They discuss how the divine presence is not just an abstract concept but something that can be experienced in daily life. Meditation, prayer, and rituals in Hindu practice are ways to connect with this divine presence, emphasizing God's immanence.

The many gods and goddesses in Hinduism also reflect different aspects of Brahman. Each deity represents a different facet of the divine, from creation and destruction to love and wisdom. This diversity within unity is a key feature of panentheistic belief, showing how the divine can be both one and many.

Hinduism provides a rich framework for understanding panentheism. It offers a vision of a universe filled with divine presence, where everything is interconnected and sacred. This perspective encourages a deep reverence for life and the world around us.

BUDDHISM AND PANENTHEISTIC ELEMENTS

While often seen as a non-theistic religion, Buddhism contains elements that resonate with panentheism. Central to Buddhist thought is the concept of interdependence, which suggests that all things are connected. This idea aligns with the panentheistic view that the divine presence permeates the universe.

In Mahayana Buddhism, the idea of Buddha-nature suggests that all beings have the potential to achieve enlightenment. This concept implies a divine essence within each person, similar to the panentheistic belief in the immanence of God. It encourages the view that the sacred is present within every individual.

Buddhist practices such as meditation and mindfulness aim to cultivate awareness of this interconnectedness. By recognizing the interdependent nature of reality, practitioners can develop a deeper understanding of the divine presence in all things. This perspective encourages compassion and empathy, as all beings are seen as part of the same spiritual fabric.

The concept of Emptiness (Sunyata) in Buddhism also has panentheistic implications. It suggests that all phenomena are empty of inherent existence but are filled with the potential for divine presence. This paradoxical idea reflects the panentheistic view of a dynamic and evolving universe where the divine is both immanent and transcendent.

While Buddhism does not explicitly endorse a concept of God, its emphasis on interdependence, Buddha-nature, and Emptiness provides a framework for understanding the divine presence in the world. These ideas contribute to a broader panentheistic perspective that sees the sacred in all aspects of life.

TAOISM AND THE DIVINE

Taoism, an ancient Chinese philosophy and religion, offers a unique perspective on the divine that aligns closely with panentheism. Central to Taoist thought is the concept of the Tao, often translated as "the Way." The Tao is seen as the fundamental principle that underlies and unites all of reality. It is both immanent, present in every aspect of the world, and transcendent, beyond all human comprehension.

The Tao is described as the source of all creation, giving life and order to the universe. This idea mirrors the panentheistic view that the divine is the origin of everything, present within the world yet extending beyond it. The Tao's presence in all things encourages a sense of harmony and balance, key aspects of panentheistic thought.

In Taoism, practices such as meditation, Tai Chi, and Qigong are ways to align oneself with the Tao. These practices aim to cultivate an awareness of the divine presence within and around us. By living in harmony with the Tao, individuals can achieve a sense of balance and peace, reflecting the immanence of the divine in daily life.

Taoist texts like the Tao Te Ching and the Zhuangzi explore these ideas in poetic and philosophical terms. They emphasize the interconnectedness of all things and the importance of living following the natural order. This perspective encourages a deep reverence for nature and the recognition of the divine in the world around us.

Taoism provides a rich and nuanced understanding of the divine that aligns well with panentheistic principles. It offers a vision of a universe filled with the presence of the Tao, where everything is interconnected and sacred. This perspective encourages a holistic and harmonious approach to life.

SHINTO BELIEFS

Shinto, the indigenous religion of Japan, also contains elements that resonate with panentheism. Central to Shinto belief is the concept of kami, which are spirits or divine beings present in nature. Kami can be found in mountains, rivers, trees, and even objects and people. This idea reflects the panentheistic view that the divine is immanent in the world.

In Shinto, the natural world is seen as sacred, filled with the presence of kami. This perspective encourages a deep reverence for nature and a recognition of the divine in all aspects of life. Shinto practices such as purification rituals, offerings, and festivals are ways to honor and connect with the kami.

The concept of musubi, or the creative and harmonizing power, is also central to Shinto belief. Musubi reflects the dynamic and evolving nature of the divine presence, aligning with the panentheistic view of a universe in constant interaction with the divine. This idea emphasizes the interconnectedness of all things and the importance of maintaining harmony.

Shinto shrines, built to honor kami, serve as places of worship and reflection. These shrines are often located in natural settings, reinforcing the connection between the divine and the natural world. The practice of visiting shrines encourages a sense of awe and reverence for nature's sacredness.

Shinto offers a unique and rich perspective on the divine that aligns closely with panentheistic principles. It provides a vision of a world filled with the presence of kami, where everything is interconnected and sacred. This perspective encourages a deep respect for nature and recognizing the divine in all aspects of life.

COMPARATIVE ANALYSIS

Comparing the expressions of panentheism in Hinduism, Buddhism, Taoism, and Shinto reveals both common themes and unique perspectives. Each tradition emphasizes the presence of the divine in the world, but they approach this idea in different ways. This diversity enriches our under-standing of panentheism and highlights its universal appeal.

In Hinduism, the concept of Brahman as the ultimate reality that pervades everything aligns closely with panentheism. The idea of Atman, or the individual soul, as part of Brahman reflects the interconnectedness of all things. This perspective emphasizes the immanence of the divine and the sacredness of life.

Buddhism, with its emphasis on interdependence and Buddha nature, also resonates with panentheistic principles. The idea that all beings have the potential for enlightenment suggests a divine presence within each individual. This perspective encourages compassion and the recognition of the sacred in everyday life.

Taoism offers a unique perspective with its concept of the Tao, the fundamental principle that underlies and unites all of reality. The Tao's immanence and transcendence reflect the panentheistic view of a dynamic and evolving divine presence. This perspective emphasizes harmony and balance in life.

Shinto's focus on the kami, spirits present in nature, high-lights the immanence of the divine in the world. The concept of musubi, the creative and harmonizing power, reflects the dynamic nature of the divine presence. This perspective encourages a deep reverence for nature and recognition of the sacred in all aspects of life.

Comparing these traditions reveals common themes of interconnectedness, immanence, and the sacredness of life. Each tradition offers unique insights and practices that enrich our understanding of panentheism. This comparative analysis highlights the universal appeal of panentheistic thought and its relevance to diverse spiritual traditions.

MODERN INTERPRETATIONS

Modern interpretations of panentheism in Eastern religions continue to evolve, influenced by contemporary spiritual, philosophical, and scientific insights. These interpretations build on traditional teachings while adapting to new contexts and challenges, reflecting panentheistic thought's dynamic and evolving nature.

In Hinduism, modern interpretations of panentheism emphasize the integration of spirituality and science. Recognizing the interconnectedness of all things aligns with scientific discoveries in fields like quantum physics and ecology. This perspective encourages a holistic approach to spirituality, where scientific and spiritual insights complement each other.

Buddhist teachings on interdependence and mindfulness have gained widespread popularity today. These practices encourage a deep awareness of the present moment and the recognition of the interconnectedness of all life. Modern interpretations of Buddhist panentheism emphasize the relevance of these teachings for addressing contemporary issues such as stress, mental health, and environmental sustainability.

Taoism's emphasis on harmony and balance continues to inspire modern spiritual practices. People around the world embrace practices such as Tai Chi, Qigong, and meditation to cultivate physical, mental, and spiritual well-being. Modern interpretations of Taoist panentheism emphasize the importance of living in harmony with nature and the interconnectedness of all things.

Shinto's focus on the sacredness of nature resonates with contemporary environmental concerns. Modern interpretations of Shinto panentheism emphasize the importance of ecological stewardship and the recognition of the divine presence in the natural world. This perspective encourages a deep reverence for the environment and sustainable living practices.

Modern interpretations of panentheism in Eastern religions reflect the adaptability and relevance of these teachings. They build on traditional wisdom while addressing contemporary challenges, offering rich and diverse perspectives on the divine and the interconnectedness of all life. These interpretations enrich our understanding of panentheism and its relevance to the modern world.

PANENTHEISM IN WESTERN RELIGIONS

CHRISTIANITY AND PANENTHEISM

With its rich theological tradition, Christianity has various interpretations that align with panentheism. One prominent example is the concept of the Holy Spirit. In Christian theology, the Holy Spirit is seen as God's presence in the world, actively involved in the lives of believers. This idea fits well with panentheism, where the divine is both within and beyond the universe.

Many Christian mystics, such as Julian of Norwich and Meister Eckhart, wrote about their experiences of God in a way that reflects panentheistic thought. They described a God who is deeply intertwined with the world yet transcends it. Their writings emphasize God's immanence in all creation, suggesting a divine presence that permeates everything.

The idea of the Incarnation, where God became human in the form of Jesus Christ, also has panentheistic elements. It suggests that the divine can fully inhabit the material world, breaking down the barrier between the sacred and the secular. This belief highlights the possibility of encountering the divine in everyday life.

Some theologians advocate for a panentheistic view to address modern scientific understanding and ecological concerns in contemporary Christianity. They argue that seeing God as immanent in creation fosters a deeper respect for the environment and a sense of interconnectedness. This approach encourages Christians to engage with the world in a way that honors its divine presence.

Christianity provides a rich context for exploring panentheistic ideas. It offers a vision of a God intimately connected to creation, encouraging believers to see the sacred in all aspects of life. This perspective can deepen one's spiritual practice and understanding.

JEWISH MYSTICISM (KABBALAH)

Jewish mysticism, particularly Kabbalah, offers profound insights into panentheistic thought. Kabbalistic teachings explore the nature of God and the universe in ways that resonate with panentheism. Central to Kabbalah is the idea of Ein Sof, the infinite and unknowable aspect of God that permeates all existence. This concept aligns with the panentheistic view of a divine presence that is both immanent and transcendent.

The Kabbalistic Tree of Life, a symbolic representation of the divine emanations, illustrates how God interacts with the world. Each emanation, or Sephirah, reflects a different aspect of the divine, suggesting a multifaceted and interconnected view of God. This structure emphasizes the dynamic relationship between the divine and the material world.

Kabbalistic texts, such as the Zohar, delve into mystical experiences that reveal the presence of God in all things. These writings describe moments of profound spiritual insight where the boundaries between the divine and the mundane blur. Such experiences highlight God's immanence and the interconnectedness of all creation.

In Jewish practice, the concept of Tikkun Olam, or "repairing the world," reflects panentheistic principles. It suggests that human actions can restore harmony and balance to the universe, aligning it with the divine will. This belief encourages a sense of responsibility and engagement with the world, seeing every action as an opportunity to reflect the divine presence.

Kabbalah continues to influence contemporary Jewish thought and spirituality. Its emphasis on the interconnectedness of all things and the immanence of the divine offers a rich framework for understanding panentheism. By exploring these mystical teachings, we gain a deeper appreciation for the sacredness of life and the divine presence within it.

ISLAMIC PERSPECTIVES (SUFISM)

Sufism, the mystical branch of Islam, offers a deeply spiritual perspective that aligns with panentheism. Central to Sufi thought is the idea that God is both immanent and transcendent, present in all aspects of creation yet beyond comprehension. Sufis seek to experience this divine presence directly through meditation, prayer, and chanting.

One of the most famous Sufi poets, Rumi, wrote extensively about the divine presence in the world. His poetry often describes a profound sense of unity with God, where the boundaries between the self and the divine dissolve. This experience of oneness reflects the panentheistic belief in the immanence of God in all things.

Sufi practices, such as Dhikr (remembrance of God), aim to cultivate an awareness of the divine presence in everyday life. By focusing on the names and attributes of God, practitioners seek to align their hearts and minds with the divine. This practice emphasizes the idea that God is always near and accessible through devotion and mindfulness.

The concept of Wahdat al-Wujud, or the "Unity of Being," is a key element of Sufi thought that resonates with panentheism. It suggests that all existence is a manifestation of the divine, and everything in the universe reflects God's presence. This perspective encourages a holistic view of life, where the sacred and the mundane are interconnected.

Sufism continues to inspire contemporary Islamic spirituality, emphasizing God's immanence and the interconnectedness of all creation. Its mystical teachings and practices offer a rich framework for understanding panentheism within the context of Islam. By exploring Sufi thought, we gain a deeper appreciation for the divine presence in the world.

PANENTHEISM IN INDIGENOUS TRADITIONS

Indigenous traditions around the world often reflect panentheistic beliefs, seeing the divine as present in nature and all

living beings. These cultures typically emphasize a deep
connection with the natural world, recognizing the sacredness of the environment and all its inhabitants. This perspective aligns closely with panentheism, where the divine
permeates all aspects of life.

In many Indigenous cultures, the Earth is viewed as a living
entity imbued with spiritual significance. The land, water,
plants, and animals are all seen as manifestations of the
divine, deserving of respect and reverence. This belief fosters
a sense of interconnectedness and responsibility for maintaining the balance and harmony of the natural world.

Rituals and ceremonies in Indigenous traditions often aim to
honor the divine presence in nature. Practices such as
offering prayers, songs, and dances are ways to connect with
the spiritual essence of the Earth. These rituals emphasize
the immanence of the divine, highlighting the sacredness of
everyday life and the world around us.

The concept of the Great Spirit or Creator is common in
many Indigenous belief systems. This divine presence is seen
as both within and beyond the physical world, guiding and
sustaining all creation. This dual aspect of the divine reflects
panentheistic principles, where God is both immanent and
transcendent.

Indigenous traditions continue to influence contemporary
spiritual practices, emphasizing the importance of living in
harmony with the Earth. Their panentheistic worldview
offers valuable insights into the interconnectedness of all life
and the sacredness of the natural world. By exploring these
traditions, we gain a deeper appreciation for the divine presence in every aspect of existence.

WESTERN MYSTICAL TRADITIONS

Western mystical traditions, including Christian mysticism, Gnosticism, and Neoplatonism, offer rich perspectives that align with panentheism. These traditions emphasize direct experiences of the divine, where the boundaries between the sacred and the secular blur. Mystics in these traditions often describe encounters with a God who is both immanent and transcendent.

Christian mystics like Julian of Norwich and Meister Eckhart wrote about their experiences of God in ways that reflected panentheistic thought. They described a divine presence that permeates all creation, suggesting that God is deeply intertwined with the world. Their writings emphasize God's immanence, encouraging believers to seek the divine in everyday life.

Gnosticism, an early Christian movement, also contains elements of panentheism. Gnostic texts describe a divine spark within each individual, connecting them to the larger cosmic reality. This belief in the immanence of the divine within the self aligns with panentheistic principles, suggesting a deep interconnectedness of all things.

Neoplatonism, a philosophical tradition that emerged in the 3rd century, offers a panentheistic view of the divine. Plotinus, the founder of Neoplatonism, described the One as the ultimate source of all existence, present in everything yet beyond comprehension. This idea reflects the panentheistic belief in a God who is both immanent and transcendent.

Western mystical traditions continue to influence contemporary spiritual thought, emphasizing the interconnectedness of all life and the immanence of the divine. These mystical teachings offer a rich framework for understanding panentheism, encouraging a deeper exploration of the divine presence in the world. By engaging with these traditions, we gain valuable insights into the nature of the sacred and our relationship with the divine.

THEOLOGICAL DEBATES

Theological debates around panentheism often center on its implications for traditional religious beliefs. One key debate is the distinction between panentheism and pantheism. While both views see the divine as present in the world, panentheism maintains that God also transcends the universe. This dual aspect of the divine challenges simple definitions and invites deeper exploration.

Another debate focuses on the implications of panentheism for the nature of God. Traditional theism often views God as a separate, all-powerful being. Panentheism, however, suggests a more dynamic relationship between the divine and the world. This perspective raises questions about God's role in creation and the nature of divine power.

Panentheism also prompts discussions about the problem of evil. If God is immanent, how do we account for suffering and injustice? Some theologians argue that panentheism offers a more compassionate view of God, emphasizing divine empathy and engagement with the world. Others question whether this view adequately addresses the reality of evil.

The relationship between science and religion is another area of debate. Panentheism's emphasis on the interconnectedness of all things resonates with scientific discoveries in fields like quantum physics and ecology. This alignment encourages a dialogue between science and spirituality, challenging traditional boundaries and fostering a holistic understanding of the universe.

CONTEMPORARY RELIGIOUS PRACTICES

Contemporary religious practices that incorporate panentheism emphasize the presence of the divine in everyday life. These practices often blend traditional rituals with modern insights, creating a dynamic and evolving spiritual experience. They encourage believers to see the sacred in all aspects of life, fostering a deeper connection with the divine.

In Christianity, some churches emphasize ecological stewardship as a form of spiritual practice. This approach reflects panentheistic principles, recognizing the divine presence in nature and encouraging sustainable living. Practices such as community gardens, eco-friendly worship services, and environmental activism are ways to honor the divine in the natural world.

Jewish communities that embrace Kabbalistic teachings often incorporate meditation and mindfulness practices into their religious observances. These practices aim to cultivate an awareness of the divine presence within and around us. They encourage a holistic approach to spirituality, where everyday actions are seen as opportunities to connect with the divine.

Sufi communities continue to practice traditional rituals such as Dhikr and Whirling Dervishes, emphasizing God's immanence in all things. These practices foster a deep sense of unity with the divine, encouraging believers to experience

God's presence in every moment. They reflect the panenthe-istic view that the sacred is present in all aspects of life.

Indigenous spiritual practices that emphasize the sacredness of nature continue to inspire contemporary religious move-ments. These practices often include rituals that honor the Earth and its inhabitants, fostering a deep reverence for the natural world. They reflect a panentheistic worldview that sees the divine in every part of creation.

PANENTHEISM IN PHILOSOPHY

PHILOSOPHICAL UNDERPINNINGS

The philosophical underpinnings of panentheism are both deep and broad, stretching back to ancient times. At its core, panentheism posits that the divine is both immanent in the world and transcends it. This idea challenges the traditional view of God as entirely separate from creation. Instead, it suggests a more interconnected relationship between the divine and the universe.

One of the key philosophical questions in panentheism is how the divine can be present in all things while also existing beyond them. This dual aspect of immanence and transcendence requires a nuanced understanding of the nature of existence. Philosophers have debated whether this view implies that the world is a part of God or that God is a part of the world.

The idea of interconnectedness is also central to panentheism. This concept suggests that everything in the universe is linked through the divine presence. It implies a holistic view of reality, where every part reflects the whole. This perspective challenges the dualistic thinking that separates the sacred from the secular.

Another important aspect of panentheism is its dynamic view of the divine. Unlike static concepts of God, panentheism sees the divine as actively engaged with the world. This ongoing interaction reflects the evolving nature of the universe and the divine presence within it. It suggests that creation is a continuous process influenced by the divine.

Panentheism's philosophical underpinnings offer a rich and complex framework for understanding the divine and its relationship with the world. By exploring these foundational ideas, we gain a deeper appreciation for the interconnectedness and dynamic nature of existence.

CONTRIBUTIONS OF PLATO AND ARISTOTLE

Plato and Aristotle, two of the most influential philosophers in Western thought, contributed significantly to ideas that resonate with panentheism. Plato's concept of the World Soul is one such idea. He proposed that the World Soul is an animating force that permeates the entire universe. This notion aligns with the panentheistic view of a divine presence within all things.

Plato's theory of forms also contributes to panentheistic thought. He believed that the physical world reflected a higher, more perfect reality. This idea suggests a connection between the material and the divine, where the world we experience is infused with a deeper spiritual essence. This perspective encourages us to see the sacred in the everyday.

On the other hand, Aristotle introduced the Prime Mover concept. He described it as the ultimate cause of all motion and change in the universe. The Prime Mover, while not directly involved in the world, is still the source of all activity. This idea hints at a transcendent force that underlies and sustains the physical world, a key aspect of panentheism.

Aristotle's notion of the Prime Mover differs from traditional theism in that it does not depict a God who intervenes in human affairs. Instead, it presents a divine force that sets the universe in motion and sustains it. This view aligns with panentheism's emphasis on the interconnectedness and ongoing interaction between the divine and the world.

Plato and Aristotle laid the groundwork for later philosophical developments that align with panentheistic thought. Their ideas about the World Soul and the Prime Mover offer rich insights into the nature of the divine and its relationship with the universe. By building on their contributions, we can deepen our understanding of panentheism.

INFLUENCE OF PLOTINUS

Plotinus, a philosopher of the 3rd century, played a crucial role in the development of panentheistic ideas. He founded Neoplatonism, a philosophical system that built on Plato's ideas. Central to Plotinus's thought is the concept of the One, an ultimate reality that transcends all existence. The One is the source of everything, and everything is connected to it.

Plotinus described the process of emanation, in which all levels of reality flow from the One. This process suggests that the divine presence permeates all levels of existence, from the highest spiritual realms to the material world. This idea aligns closely with panentheism, in which the divine is both immanent in the world and beyond it.

The notion of return is also key to Plotinus's philosophy. He believed that all beings naturally desire to return to the One. This idea suggests a dynamic relationship between the divine and the world, where creation is constantly drawn back to its source. This perspective emphasizes the interconnectedness and unity of all things.

Plotinus's mystical experiences further illustrate his panentheistic views. He described moments of profound union with the One, where the boundaries between the self and the divine dissolve. These experiences highlight the immanence of the divine and the potential for direct encounters with the sacred in everyday life.

Plotinus's influence extends beyond his time, impacting later philosophical and theological thought. His ideas about the One, emanation, and return provide a rich framework for understanding the nature of the divine and its relationship with the world. We gain deeper insights into the panentheistic vision of existence by exploring Plotinus's contributions.

MODERN PHILOSOPHICAL THINKERS

Modern philosophical thinkers have continued to explore and expand on panentheistic ideas. One such thinker is Alfred North Whitehead, a British philosopher known for developing process philosophy. Whitehead's view of the universe as a series of interconnected processes resonates with panentheistic thought. He proposed that God is immanent in these processes and transcendent, guiding their evolution.

Another influential figure is Pierre Teilhard de Chardin, a French Jesuit priest and paleontologist. Teilhard de Chardin's concept of the Omega Point suggests that the universe is evolving toward a higher state of consciousness and unity with the divine. This idea reflects the dynamic and interconnected nature of panentheism, where the divine presence guides the unfolding of the cosmos.

Philosopher Charles Hartshorne also made significant contributions to panentheistic thought. He developed the idea of process theology, which emphasizes God's dynamic and relational nature. Hartshorne's view that God is affected by and responsive to the world aligns with the panentheistic belief in a divine presence actively engaged with creation.

Contemporary philosopher Jürgen Moltmann has explored panentheistic themes in his work on eco-theology. Moltmann argues that seeing God as immanent in nature can foster a deeper respect for the environment. This perspective encourages a holistic view of life, where all aspects of existence are interconnected and sacred.

These modern thinkers have enriched the philosophical landscape with their explorations of panentheism. By building on traditional ideas and integrating contemporary insights, they offer fresh perspectives on the divine and its relationship with the world. Their contributions continue to inspire and inform our understanding of panentheism.

PANENTHEISM AND METAPHYSICS

Panentheism has significant implications for metaphysics, the branch of philosophy that explores the nature of reality. At its core, panentheism challenges the traditional dualism that separates the divine from the material world. Instead, it posits a more interconnected and holistic view of existence, where the divine permeates all aspects of reality.

One key metaphysical question in panentheism is the nature of being. Panentheism suggests that all beings are expressions of the divine presence, connected to a larger spiritual reality. This perspective emphasizes the unity and diversity of existence, where every part reflects the whole. It encourages us to see the sacred in all things.

Another important aspect of panentheistic metaphysics is the idea of process and change. Unlike static views of reality, panentheism sees the universe as dynamic and evolving. The divine presence guides this ongoing process, reflecting a continuous interaction between the sacred and the material world. This view challenges fixed notions of being and encourages a more fluid understanding of existence.

The concept of relationality is also central to panentheistic metaphysics. It suggests that all things are interconnected through the divine presence, forming a web of relationships. This perspective highlights the importance of context and connection in understanding the nature of reality. It challenges isolated views of existence and emphasizes the interdependence of all things.

Panentheism offers a rich and complex metaphysical framework for understanding the nature of reality. By exploring these foundational ideas, we gain deeper insights into the interconnectedness and dynamic nature of existence. Panentheistic metaphysics encourages a holistic view of life, where the divine presence permeates all aspects of reality.

EPISTEMOLOGICAL CONSIDERATIONS

Epistemology, the study of knowledge, is deeply influenced by panentheistic thought. One key question is how we come to know the divine presence in the world. Panentheism suggests that the divine can be experienced directly through everyday life, challenging the notion that spiritual knowledge is separate from ordinary experience.

This perspective emphasizes the role of intuition and mystical experience in knowing the divine. Panentheism posits that moments of deep connection and insight reveal the immanence of the divine in the world. These experiences highlight the interconnectedness of all things and provide a direct encounter with the sacred.

Panentheism also challenges the dualistic thinking that separates the knower from the known. It suggests that knowledge is relational, formed through interactions with the world and its divine presence. This perspective encourages a holistic view of knowledge, where understanding is rooted in context and connection.

The role of community is another important aspect of panentheistic epistemology. It suggests that spiritual knowledge is not just an individual pursuit but a collective endeavor. By engaging with others and sharing experiences, we deepen our understanding of the divine and its presence in the world. This communal approach highlights the interconnected nature of knowledge.

Panentheism offers a rich and nuanced framework for understanding how we come to know the divine. It emphasizes the importance of direct experience, relational knowledge, and community in pursuing spiritual understanding. By exploring these epistemological considerations, we gain deeper insights into the nature of knowledge and the divine presence in the world.

ETHICAL DIMENSIONS

The ethical dimensions of panentheism are profound and far-reaching. Panentheism suggests that because the divine is present in all things, our actions directly impact the sacred. This perspective encourages a deep sense of responsibility and care for the world around us, highlighting the interconnectedness of all life.

One key ethical implication of panentheism is the responsibility to care for the environment. By recognizing the divine presence in nature, we are encouraged to treat the Earth with respect and reverence. This perspective fosters a sense of stewardship, where protecting the environment is seen as a form of spiritual practice.

Panentheism also emphasizes the importance of compassion and empathy. Seeing the divine in all beings encourages us to treat others with kindness and respect. This ethical framework promotes social justice and the well-being of all individuals, reflecting the interconnected nature of existence.

Another important ethical dimension is the emphasis on holistic living. Panentheism suggests that ethical behavior is not limited to specific actions but encompasses our entire way of life. This perspective encourages us to live harmoniously with the divine presence in all things, integrating spirituality and ethics into our daily lives.

Panentheism's ethical dimensions offer a rich and nuanced framework for living a compassionate and responsible life. By recognizing the interconnectedness and sacredness of all life, we are guided toward ethical behavior that respects and honors the divine presence in the world. This perspective fosters a sense of purpose and responsibility, enriching our spiritual and ethical understanding.

SCIENTIFIC PERSPECTIVES

INTERSECTION OF SCIENCE AND THEOLOGY

The relationship between science and theology has always been complex. Panentheism, however, offers a bridge between these two fields. It suggests that the divine is present in all things, making studying the natural world a way to understand God. This perspective encourages a dialogue between scientific discoveries and spiritual insights.

One key area of intersection is the idea of interconnectedness. Science shows us that everything in the universe is connected, from the smallest particles to the largest galaxies. Panentheism mirrors this view by positing that the divine presence permeates all existence. This alignment suggests that scientific exploration can deepen our spiritual understanding.

Another important aspect is the dynamic nature of reality. Scientific theories, such as those in physics and biology, describe a universe in constant change and evolution. Panentheism also sees the divine as actively engaged in the ongoing creation process. This dynamic view supports the idea that God is involved in the continuous unfolding of the cosmos.

Ethics is another area where science and theology intersect in panentheism. Scientific advancements raise important ethical questions, such as those related to the environment and human well-being. Panentheism's emphasis on the sacredness of all life provides a moral framework for addressing these issues. It encourages us to consider the divine presence in all our actions and decisions.

Panentheism's intersection of science and theology offers a rich and nuanced understanding of the world. By seeing the divine in all things, we can integrate scientific knowledge with spiritual wisdom, enriching both our scientific inquiries and our spiritual practices.

QUANTUM PHYSICS AND PANENTHEISM

Quantum physics has revolutionized our understanding of the universe. It reveals a world that is deeply interconnected and full of mysteries. Panentheism finds a natural ally in quantum physics, as both suggest a reality where everything is linked through a deeper, unseen connection. This alignment offers fascinating insights into the nature of existence.

One key concept in quantum physics is entanglement, where particles become interconnected in such a way that the state of one instantly influences the state of another, no matter the distance between them. This phenomenon suggests a level of connectivity that aligns with panentheistic thought. It implies a universe where the divine presence is intimately woven into the fabric of reality.

Another intriguing idea is the role of the observer in quantum physics. Experiments have shown that the act of observation can affect the outcome of quantum events. This suggests that consciousness plays a significant role in shaping reality. Panentheism, which sees the divine in all aspects of existence, resonates with this view by suggesting that human consciousness can interact with and reflect the divine presence.

Quantum physics also challenges the traditional notion of a deterministic universe. Instead, it presents a reality full of probabilities and potentialities. Panentheism embraces this dynamic view of the cosmos, where the divine presence guides and influences the unfolding of events. This perspective encourages us to see the world as a place of endless possibilities and divine interaction.

The mysterious and interconnected nature of quantum physics invites a sense of wonder and reverence. It challenges us to rethink our understanding of reality and our place within it. Panentheism, emphasizing the divine presence in all things, provides a framework for integrating these scientific insights with spiritual understanding.

COSMOLOGY AND CREATION

Cosmology, the study of the origins and structure of the universe, offers profound insights that resonate with panentheism. It explores questions about the beginning of the cosmos and its ultimate fate, areas where science and theology often intersect. Panentheism provides a framework for seeing these cosmic processes as expressions of the divine presence.

The Big Bang Theory, which describes the universe's origin, aligns with the panentheistic view of a dynamic and evolving creation. According to this theory, the universe began as a singular point and has expanded ever since. Panentheism sees this expansion as a manifestation of the divine presence, continually unfolding and creating new possibilities.

Cosmology also reveals the intricate structure of the universe, from galaxies and stars to planets and life forms. This complexity suggests a level of order and purpose that resonates with the panentheistic belief in a divine presence guiding the cosmos. It encourages us to see the universe as a sacred space filled with the divine in every part.

Another important aspect of cosmology is the concept of dark matter and dark energy, which make up most of the universe yet remain largely mysterious. These unknown aspects of the cosmos invite a sense of awe and wonder, similar to the panentheistic view of the divine as both immanent and transcendent. They remind us that there is always more to discover about the nature of existence.

The study of cosmology challenges us to consider our place in the universe. Panentheism encourages us to see ourselves as part of a larger, interconnected whole, where every action reflects the divine presence. This perspective fosters a sense of responsibility and reverence for the cosmos and all its inhabitants.

EVOLUTION AND DIVINE PRESENCE

The theory of evolution provides a scientific explanation for the diversity of life on Earth. It describes a process of gradual change and adaptation over millions of years. Panentheism embraces this dynamic view of life, seeing evolution as a way through which the divine presence is expressed and realized in the world.

One of the key aspects of evolution is the idea of common descent, which suggests that all living organisms share a common ancestor. This interconnectedness aligns with the panentheistic view of a universe where everything is linked through the divine presence. It encourages us to see all life as part of a sacred, interconnected web.

Natural selection, a driving force in evolution, emphasizes the adaptability and resilience of life. Panentheism sees this process as a reflection of the divine presence, guiding and sustaining the unfolding of life. It suggests that the divine is actively involved in the creation process, continuously bringing forth new forms of life and possibilities.

The complexity and diversity of life on Earth reveal a level of creativity that resonates with panentheistic thought. From the intricate structure of a cell to the vast ecosystems of the planet, every aspect of life reflects the divine presence. This perspective encourages a deep appreciation for the beauty and wonder of the natural world.

Evolution also challenges us to rethink our understanding of humanity's place in the world. Panentheism suggests that humans are part of the larger web of life, connected to all other forms of existence through the divine presence. This view fosters a sense of humility and responsibility, encouraging us to live in harmony with the rest of creation.

THE ROLE OF CONSCIOUSNESS

Consciousness, the state of being aware and able to think, is one of the most profound and mysterious aspects of human experience. Panentheism sees consciousness as a reflection of the divine presence within us. It suggests that our awareness and ability to think are ways through which we connect with the divine.

One of the key questions in the study of consciousness is how it arises from the physical brain. Panentheism offers a perspective where consciousness is not just a product of physical processes but also a manifestation of the divine presence. This view suggests that our awareness is deeply connected to the spiritual dimension of existence.

The idea of collective consciousness, where individuals' awareness is connected to a larger whole, resonates with panentheistic thought. It suggests that our thoughts and experiences are part of a greater, interconnected web of divine presence. This perspective encourages a sense of unity and shared purpose among all beings.

Consciousness also plays a significant role in shaping our understanding of reality. Panentheism suggests that our awareness allows us to perceive the divine presence in the world. It encourages us to cultivate mindfulness and spiritual practices that deepen our connection to the divine. This view sees consciousness as a bridge between the physical and spiritual realms.

Exploring the nature of consciousness challenges us to consider the deeper aspects of our existence. Panentheism offers a framework for understanding consciousness as a reflection of the divine presence within us. This perspective enriches our spiritual practice and understanding, encouraging us to explore the mysteries of awareness and existence.

ENVIRONMENTAL SCIENCE AND PANENTHEISM

Environmental science studies the natural world and the impact of human activities on it. Panentheism, emphasizing the divine presence in all things, offers a valuable perspective for understanding and addressing environmental issues. It suggests that caring for the environment is a form of spiritual practice, reflecting the sacredness of the natural world.

One of the key insights from environmental science is the interconnectedness of ecosystems. This concept aligns with the panentheistic view of a universe where everything is linked through the divine presence. It encourages us to see the natural world as a sacred web of life deserving of respect and protection.

Climate change, one of the most pressing environmental issues, challenges us to rethink our relationship with the planet. Panentheism suggests that the divine presence is affected by the well-being of the Earth. This perspective fosters a sense of responsibility and urgency in addressing environmental degradation, seeing it as a spiritual and moral issue.

Sustainable living practices, such as reducing waste and conserving resources, reflect panentheistic principles. They encourage us to live in harmony with the natural world, recognizing the divine presence in all aspects of life. These practices offer practical ways to honor the sacredness of the environment and contribute to its protection.

Environmental science also highlights the importance of biodiversity and the variety of life on Earth. Panentheism sees this diversity as a reflection of the divine presence, expressing the creativity and abundance of the sacred. This perspective encourages a deep appreciation for the richness of life and the need to preserve it.

The intersection of environmental science and panentheism offers a rich framework for understanding and addressing environmental issues. By seeing the divine in all things, we are encouraged to live in ways that honor and protect the natural world. This holistic approach enriches both our scientific understanding and our spiritual practice.

FUTURE SCIENTIFIC DEVELOPMENTS

The future of scientific discovery holds immense potential for deepening our understanding of the universe. Panentheism, emphasizing the divine presence in all things, provides a framework for integrating these discoveries with spiritual insights. This perspective encourages a holistic view of science and spirituality, where each informs and enriches the other.

One area of future development is the exploration of the cosmos. Advances in space exploration and technology will likely reveal new insights into the structure and origins of the universe. Panentheism suggests that these discoveries will further illuminate the divine presence in the cosmos, deepening our sense of wonder and connection.

Another exciting field is biotechnology, which holds the promise of transforming our understanding of life and health. Panentheism encourages us to approach these advancements with a sense of reverence and responsibility. By recognizing the divine presence in all living beings, we can ensure that biotechnological developments honor the sacredness of life.

Artificial intelligence and machine learning are also areas of rapid growth and innovation. These technologies challenge us to consider the nature of consciousness and intelligence. Panentheism offers a perspective where artificial forms of intelligence can reflect the divine presence, inviting us to explore the spiritual implications of these advancements.

Environmental science will continue to play a crucial role in addressing global challenges. Panentheism suggests that future developments in this field will further highlight the interconnectedness of all life. By integrating scientific insights with spiritual wisdom, we can develop sustainable practices that honor the divine presence in the natural world.

Future scientific developments can deepen our understanding of the universe and our place within it. Panentheism provides a valuable framework for integrating these discoveries with spiritual insights, encouraging a holistic and reverent approach to science and spirituality. By embracing this perspective, we can navigate the future with a sense of wonder, responsibility, and connection to the divine.

PANENTHEISM AND ECOLOGY

THEOLOGICAL BASIS FOR ENVIRONMENTALISM

The connection between panentheism and environmentalism starts with the idea that the divine is present in all aspects of the natural world. If we see the Earth as infused with the presence of the divine, it becomes clear why we must treat it with respect and care. This theological basis forms a strong foundation for environmentalism, providing a spiritual reason to protect and preserve the environment.

Many religious traditions emphasize stewardship, the idea that humans are caretakers of the Earth. In a panentheistic view, this role takes on even greater significance. Since the divine is immanent in all creation, harming the environment is seen as disrespecting the divine itself. This perspective encourages a sense of sacred duty toward environmental conservation.

Scriptures and religious teachings often support this view. For instance, many biblical passages speak of the Earth as God's creation, meant to be cherished and safeguarded. Similar sentiments can be found in other religious texts, suggesting a universal recognition of the sacredness of nature. These teachings can inspire and guide environmental action among the faithful.

Religious leaders and communities have increasingly embraced environmentalism as a moral imperative. By framing ecological issues in terms of spiritual duty, they motivate individuals to take action. This approach not only raises awareness but also fosters a deeper, more personal commitment to environmental causes.

The theological basis for environmentalism rooted in panentheism is powerful because it aligns spiritual beliefs with ecological practices. It transforms how people think about their relationship with the Earth, encouraging actions that honor the divine presence in nature. This perspective can lead to more sustainable and compassionate environmental practices.

GAIA THEORY

The Gaia Theory, proposed by scientist James Lovelock, offers a scientific perspective that resonates with panentheistic ideas. It suggests the Earth functions as a single, self-regulating system, much like a living organism. This theory aligns with the panentheistic view of an interconnected and dynamic universe, where the divine presence is active within all aspects of creation.

According to the Gaia Theory, the Earth maintains conditions suitable for life through complex interactions between its various components. These interactions resemble the way living organisms regulate their internal environments. This perspective encourages us to see the Earth not just as a collection of separate parts but as a cohesive, living whole.

The idea of the Earth as a living system has profound implications for how we treat the environment. If the planet is viewed as a living entity, then environmental damage can be seen as harm to a greater living being. This viewpoint fosters a sense of responsibility and care for the Earth, aligning with panentheistic principles.

Gaia Theory also emphasizes the importance of biodiversity. Just as a healthy organism relies on the proper functioning of all its parts, the Earth depends on a rich diversity of life to maintain balance and stability. This idea supports panentheism's emphasis on the interconnectedness of all life forms and the sacredness of every part of creation.

Integrating Gaia Theory and panentheism provides a compelling framework for environmental ethics. It combines scientific understanding with spiritual reverence, encouraging a holistic approach to ecological issues. By seeing the Earth as both a living system and a manifestation of the divine, we are inspired to protect and nurture our planet more diligently.

ECOSPIRITUALITY MOVEMENTS

Ecospirituality movements blend environmental activism with spiritual practices, drawing heavily on panentheistic principles. These movements emphasize the sacredness of nature and the interconnectedness of all life, inspiring people to engage in environmental conservation as a form of spiritual practice. This approach makes environmentalism not just a responsibility but a profound spiritual journey.

One prominent eco-spirituality movement is the Green Faith movement. It encourages religious communities to incorporate environmental stewardship into their spiritual practices. Green Faith fosters a deeper commitment to sustainable living by framing ecological care as a religious duty. This movement exemplifies how panentheistic ideas can inspire collective action for the environment.

Another example is the Earth Charter, a global initiative that outlines principles for building a just, sustainable, and peaceful world. The Earth Charter integrates ethical, spiritual, and environmental concerns, promoting a holistic view of life. It encourages individuals and communities to recognize their interdependence with the Earth and to take action to protect it.

Ecospirituality also finds expression in personal practices, such as eco-meditation and nature-based rituals. These practices help individuals connect with the divine presence in nature, fostering a sense of reverence and respect for the environment. Integrating spirituality with daily life makes people more likely to adopt sustainable habits and advocate for ecological justice.

Ecospirituality movements demonstrate the power of combining spiritual and environmental concerns. They show how panentheistic principles can inspire meaningful action for the planet. These movements address ecological issues and enrich spiritual practices, offering a holistic approach to living in harmony with the Earth.

ETHICAL RESPONSIBILITIES

Panentheism emphasizes that ethical responsibilities extend beyond human interactions, including our relationship with the natural world. If the divine presence is within all of creation, how we treat the environment reflects our respect for the divine. This perspective calls for a deep sense of responsibility toward the Earth and all its inhabitants.

One of the primary ethical responsibilities in a panentheistic framework is environmental stewardship. This means caring for the Earth in ways that preserve its health and vitality for future generations. It involves sustainable practices that minimize harm and promote the well-being of all life forms. Stewardship is not just a practical necessity but a spiritual duty.

Another key ethical responsibility is promoting biodiversity. Every species plays a role in the intricate web of life, contributing to the overall balance and health of the ecosystem. Protecting endangered species and preserving natural habitats are essential to honoring the interconnectedness and sacredness of all life.

Panentheism also calls for social justice as part of our ethical responsibilities. Environmental degradation often disproportionately affects marginalized communities. Addressing these injustices involves advocating for policies and practices that protect vulnerable populations and ensure equitable access to natural resources. This approach integrates environmental and social ethics.

Another crucial responsibility is educating others about the importance of environmental care. By raising awareness and sharing knowledge, we can inspire collective action for the planet. Education fosters a deeper understanding of the interconnectedness of all life and the ethical implications of our actions. It empowers individuals to make informed and compassionate choices.

PRACTICAL APPLICATIONS

Applying panentheistic principles to daily life involves making conscious choices that reflect respect for the divine presence in the natural world. One practical application is adopting sustainable living practices. This includes reducing waste, conserving energy, and choosing eco-friendly products. These actions minimize our ecological footprint and honor the sacredness of the Earth.

Another practical application is engaging in environmental activism. This can involve participating in community clean-up efforts, advocating for policy changes, or supporting conservation organizations. By actively protecting the environment, we embody the panentheistic principle of stewardship and demonstrate our commitment to the planet.

Gardening and growing food locally are also practical ways to connect with the divine presence in nature. These activities promote sustainability by reducing the need for transportation and packaging. They also foster a deeper appreciation for the cycles of growth and renewal, reflecting the interconnectedness of all life.

Spiritual practices that connect us with nature, such as eco-meditation or outdoor rituals, can also be powerful applications of panentheism. These practices help us cultivate a sense of reverence and mindfulness, deepening our connection to the divine presence in the natural world. They encourage us to live in harmony with the Earth and to recognize the sacred in everyday life.

By incorporating these practical applications into our lives, we can live in ways that reflect our respect for the divine presence in all things. Panentheism offers a holistic framework for integrating spiritual and environmental practices, enriching both our inner and outer worlds. These actions demonstrate our commitment to a sustainable and compassionate way of living.

CASE STUDIES

Examining case studies of communities and individuals who embody panentheistic principles in their environmental practices can provide valuable insights and inspiration. One notable example is the A Rocha organization, a Christian conservation group that integrates faith with ecological action. Rocha's projects, such as habitat restoration and environmental education, demonstrate how religious communities can engage in effective environmental stewardship.

Another case study is the Green Belt Movement in Kenya, founded by Wangari Maathai. This grassroots organization focuses on tree planting, environmental conservation, and women's empowerment. Maathai's work reflects a deep respect for the interconnectedness of all life and the divine presence in nature. Her efforts have led to the planting of millions of trees and the restoration of degraded landscapes.

In the United States, the Eco-Justice Program of the National Council of Churches works to address environmental and social justice issues. This program advocates for policies that protect the environment and promote social equity. It reflects pantheistic principles by emphasizing the inter-connectedness of environmental and human well-being.

The Findhorn Foundation in Scotland is another example of a community living out pantheistic principles. Findhorn combines spiritual practices with ecological sustainability, creating a model of holistic living. The community's initiatives include organic farming, renewable energy projects, and environmental education. Findhorn's approach demonstrates the potential for integrating spirituality and sustainability.

These case studies show how pantheistic principles can inspire meaningful environmental action. They highlight the importance of community engagement, education, and advocacy in addressing ecological challenges. By learning from these examples, we can find practical ways to incorporate pantheistic values into our own lives and communities.

FUTURE DIRECTIONS

Looking ahead, the future of pantheism and ecology involves expanding our understanding and application of these principles. One promising direction is the integration of new technologies with sustainable practices. Innovations in renewable energy, waste reduction, and sustainable agriculture offer opportunities to reduce our ecological footprint while honoring the divine presence in nature.

Another important direction is the promotion of ecological education. By integrating environmental studies into school curricula and community programs, we can foster a deeper understanding of the interconnectedness of all life. This education can inspire the next generation to take action for the planet, guided by panentheistic principles.

Climate change remains a critical challenge that requires collective action. Panentheism encourages us to see climate action as a spiritual duty, reflecting our responsibility to care for the Earth. Future efforts must include global cooperation, policy advocacy, and grassroots initiatives to mitigate the impacts of climate change and promote environmental justice.

Reconnecting with indigenous wisdom and practices is another valuable direction. Indigenous cultures have long understood the sacredness of the natural world and the importance of living in harmony with it. We can integrate traditional ecological knowledge with contemporary practices by learning from and collaborating with indigenous communities.

Finally, fostering a global eco-spirituality movement can help unite diverse religious and spiritual traditions in the common cause of environmental stewardship. By emphasizing the shared values of interconnectedness and respect for the Earth, such a movement can inspire collective action and create a more sustainable and compassionate world.

The future of panentheism and ecology is filled with potential. By embracing these directions, we can deepen our connection to the divine presence in nature and take meaningful action to protect our planet. This holistic approach offers hope and guidance for creating a just and sustainable future.

PANENTHEISM IN ART AND LITERATURE

INFLUENCE ON VISUAL ARTS

P anentheism has significantly impacted visual arts throughout history. Artists often use their work to explore the idea that the divine is present in everything. This perspective encourages them to see the world as sacred and meaningful, inspiring pieces that reflect this profound connection.

Many artists depict nature in a way that highlights its spiritual significance. Landscapes, animals, and natural elements are often portrayed with a sense of reverence and wonder. This approach suggests that the natural world is more than just scenery; it's a manifestation of the divine. These works invite viewers to appreciate the beauty and sacredness of the environment.

Abstract art also resonates with panentheistic ideas. By moving away from realistic depictions, abstract artists can explore deeper spiritual themes. Shapes, colors, and forms become tools to express the ineffable aspects of the divine that go beyond the physical world. This style allows for a more personal and interpretive engagement with the artwork.

Sacred geometry is another way artists incorporate panentheistic themes. Geometric patterns, seen in many religious and spiritual contexts, symbolize the interconnectedness of all things. These patterns can be found in mandalas, religious architecture, and even modern digital art. They remind viewers of the underlying order and harmony present in the universe.

Overall, visual arts offer a rich medium for expressing panentheistic ideas. Artists help us see the divine in the world around us through nature, abstraction, and sacred symbols. Their works encourage us to look beyond the surface and appreciate the deeper spiritual connections that unite all of existence.

PANENTHEISTIC THEMES IN LITERATURE

Literature provides a powerful way to explore and convey panentheistic ideas. Through stories, poems, and essays, writers can examine the interconnectedness of life and the presence of the divine in everyday experiences. This thematic approach allows readers to engage with spiritual concepts in a deeply personal and reflective manner.

In many works of fiction, nature is depicted as a living, breathing entity infused with divine presence. Characters often experience profound spiritual moments when they connect with the natural world. These narratives highlight the sacredness of the environment and encourage readers to see the divine in the world around them.

Poetry, with its focus on language and emotion, is particularly well-suited to expressing panentheistic themes. Poets use imagery and metaphor to convey the idea that the divine is present in all things. Their words evoke a sense of wonder and reverence, inviting readers to see the world through a spiritual lens.

Essays and philosophical writings also explore panentheistic ideas. The authors discuss the interconnectedness of life, the unity of the material and spiritual worlds, and the ethical implications of seeing the divine in everything. These works provide a thoughtful and analytical perspective on panentheism, enriching our understanding of this worldview.

Literature's ability to capture the nuances of human experience makes it an ideal medium for exploring panentheism. Through storytelling, poetry, and essays, writers can convey the profound sense of connection and sacredness that defines this spiritual perspective. Their works inspire readers to reflect on their own experiences and the divine presence in their lives.

MUSIC AND SPIRITUAL EXPRESSION

Music has always been a powerful form of spiritual expression, and panentheism finds a natural resonance in this art form. Musicians can convey the sense of interconnectedness and divine presence that characterizes panentheistic belief through melody, harmony, and rhythm. Music's ability to evoke emotion and transcend language makes it a unique and effective medium for exploring these themes.

Many musical compositions draw inspiration from nature, reflecting the panentheistic view of the natural world as a manifestation of the divine. Composers create pieces that capture the beauty and majesty of the environment, using music to evoke a sense of wonder and reverence. These works invite listeners to feel the sacredness of the world around them.

Spiritual and religious music often incorporates panentheistic ideas. Hymns, chants, and sacred songs express the belief that the divine is present in all things. These pieces are designed to connect worshippers with the divine, fostering a sense of unity and spiritual presence. They are a testament to the power of music to convey profound spiritual truths.

Contemporary music also explores panentheistic themes. Many modern artists create songs that reflect on the interconnectedness of life and the presence of the divine in everyday experiences. These works resonate with listeners who seek a deeper spiritual connection through music. These compositions have common themes of unity, love, and reverence for the natural world.

Music's ability to transcend words and touch the soul makes it a powerful medium for expressing panentheistic ideas. Through compositions inspired by nature, spiritual songs, and contemporary works, musicians help us experience the divine presence in our lives. Their music fosters a sense of connection and reverence that is central to panentheistic belief.

FILM AND MEDIA REPRESENTATION

Film and media provide dynamic platforms for exploring panentheistic themes, using visual storytelling to convey the interconnectedness of life and the divine presence in the world. Filmmakers can create powerful experiences that resonate with panentheistic ideas through imagery, dialogue, and narrative.

Many films depict nature in ways that highlight its spiritual significance. Cinematic techniques, such as sweeping landscapes and close-ups of natural details, evoke a sense of wonder and reverence for the environment. These visual choices suggest that the natural world is more than just a backdrop; it is imbued with the divine. Such films invite viewers to appreciate the beauty and sacredness of nature.

Science fiction and fantasy genres often explore panentheistic concepts. These films create worlds where the divine is immanent, present in every aspect of the universe. Characters often embark on journeys of spiritual discovery, learning about the interconnectedness of all life. These stories reflect panentheistic themes by blending the mystical with the mundane.

Documentaries focusing on environmental issues frequently incorporate panentheistic perspectives. By showcasing the intricate connections within ecosystems and the impact of human actions on the natural world, these films emphasize the sacredness of the environment. They inspire viewers to consider their own relationship with the Earth and their responsibilities toward it.

Television series and streaming content also explore panentheistic themes. Shows that explore philosophical and spiritual questions often touch on the interconnectedness of life and the presence of the divine. These narratives provide ongoing opportunities for viewers to engage with panentheistic ideas over extended periods, fostering deeper reflection.

Film and media offer rich avenues for representing panentheistic ideas. Through visual storytelling, filmmakers and content creators can convey the sense of divine presence and interconnectedness that defines this worldview. Their works inspire viewers to see the sacred in the world around them and to consider their own place within the larger tapestry of life.

SYMBOLISM AND ICONOGRAPHY

Symbolism and iconography play crucial roles in expressing panentheistic ideas in art and literature. Symbols serve as visual shorthand for complex spiritual concepts, allowing artists and writers to convey the presence of the divine in subtle and powerful ways. Through symbols, viewers and readers can connect with deeper layers of meaning.

Nature symbols are prevalent in panentheistic art and literature. Trees, rivers, mountains, and animals often represent the divine presence in the natural world. These symbols remind us of the sacredness of the environment and the interconnectedness of all life. They evoke a sense of wonder and reverence, encouraging us to see the divine in the everyday.

Geometric patterns and shapes are also significant in panentheistic symbolism. Sacred geometry, found in mandalas and religious architecture, represents the underlying order and harmony of the universe. These patterns suggest that the divine presence is woven into the very fabric of reality, reflecting the interconnectedness of all things.

Light is another powerful symbol in panentheistic art and literature. It represents the divine presence, illuminating the world and revealing hidden truths. Artists use light to create a sense of transcendence, suggesting that the divine is both immanent and beyond. This symbolism helps convey the spiritual depth of everyday experiences.

Mythological and religious symbols also find resonance in panentheistic works. Deities, heroes, and sacred objects often embody the divine presence in the world. These symbols connect contemporary audiences with ancient spiritual traditions, highlighting the timeless nature of panentheistic ideas.

Symbolism and iconography are essential tools for expressing panentheistic themes. Through nature symbols, geometric patterns, light, and mythological imagery, artists and writers convey the presence of the divine in all things. These symbols enrich our understanding and experience of the sacred, inviting us to see the interconnectedness of life.

ARTISTIC MOVEMENTS

Various artistic movements have embraced and expressed panentheistic ideas, using their unique styles and philosophies to explore the interconnectedness of life and the divine presence. These movements reflect the evolving understanding of panentheism and its influence on the art world.

The Romantic movement, for example, celebrated the beauty and power of nature, often depicting landscapes as sublime and awe-inspiring. Romantic artists saw nature as a manifestation of the divine, filled with spiritual significance. Their works invite viewers to experience the sacredness of the natural world and reflect on their connection to it.

The Symbolist movement also embraced panentheistic themes. Symbolist artists and writers used symbolic imagery to convey deeper spiritual truths. They believed that art could reveal the hidden, divine aspects of reality. Using mythological and mystical symbols, they sought to express the interconnectedness of all things and the presence of the divine.

Abstract Expressionism, emerging in the 20th century, explored the spiritual dimensions of art through non-representational forms. Artists like Jackson Pollock and Mark Rothko used color, shape, and movement to evoke emotional and spiritual responses. Their works suggest that the divine cannot be fully captured through realistic imagery but can be felt and experienced on a deeper level.

Contemporary environmental art often reflects panentheistic principles. Artists create works that highlight the beauty and fragility of the natural world, encouraging viewers to consider their relationship with the environment. These pieces often use natural materials and site-specific installations to emphasize the interconnectedness of life and the sacredness of the Earth.

Artistic movements have played a significant role in exploring and expressing panentheistic ideas. Through Romanticism, Symbolism, Abstract Expressionism, and environmental art, artists have used their creativity to highlight the divine presence in the world. These movements enrich our understanding of panentheism and inspire us to see the sacred in all aspects of life.

ANALYSIS OF KEY WORKS

Analyzing key works of art and literature that embody panentheistic themes can deepen our understanding of how these ideas are expressed. One notable example is William Wordsworth's poem "Tintern Abbey." In this work, Wordsworth reflects on his spiritual connection with nature. He describes the landscape as infused with a divine presence, suggesting that the natural world is a source of spiritual renewal and insight.

Another significant work is Vincent van Gogh's painting "Starry Night." This iconic piece depicts a swirling night sky filled with stars, evoking a sense of wonder and transcendence. Van Gogh's use of color and movement suggests that the universe is alive with divine energy. The painting invites viewers to see the night sky as a manifestation of the sacred.

Ralph Waldo Emerson's essay "Nature" is foundational for understanding panentheism in literature. Emerson explores the idea that the divine can be found in the natural world and nature reflects the divine spirit. His writing encourages readers to seek spiritual connection through their experiences with nature, emphasizing the interconnectedness of all life.

In music, Ludwig van Beethoven's Symphony No. 6, known as the "Pastoral Symphony," reflects panentheistic themes. This symphony captures the beauty and tranquility of the countryside, evoking a sense of harmony with nature. Beethoven's music suggests that the natural world is filled with divine presence, offering listeners a spiritual experience through sound.

Contemporary works like Terrence Malick's film "The Tree of Life" also explore panentheistic ideas. The film weaves together the story of a family with the larger narrative of the universe's creation and evolution. It suggests that the divine is present in both the intimate moments of human life and the vast processes of the cosmos. The film invites viewers to see the interconnectedness of all things and the sacredness of existence.

Analyzing these key works shows how artists and writers have used their mediums to express panentheistic themes. Their works highlight the divine presence in nature, the interconnectedness of life, and the sacredness of everyday experiences. These pieces enrich our understanding of panentheism and inspire us to see the world through a spiritual lens.

MYSTICISM AND SPIRITUALITY

MYSTICAL EXPERIENCES

Mystical experiences are profound moments when individuals feel a deep connection with the divine. They often come unexpectedly and leave a lasting impact on the person. They can happen in nature, prayer, or everyday activities. People describe these moments as a sense of unity with all that exists.

One of the most common features of mystical experiences is the feeling of oneness. Those who have these experiences often report feeling that they are a part of something much larger than themselves. This can bring a sense of peace and understanding that is hard to put into words. It's as if the boundaries between themselves and the world around them dissolve.

Mystical experiences also tend to involve a heightened sense of reality. Colors might appear brighter, sounds clearer, and emotions more intense. This heightened awareness makes everything feel more alive and interconnected. It's as though the divine presence is shining through every part of the world.

These experiences can be life-changing. People often come away from them with a new perspective on life and a deeper sense of purpose. They may feel more connected to others and more compassionate. These moments can also inspire a greater appreciation for the beauty and mystery of the world.

PRACTICES AND RITUALS

Practices and rituals play a crucial role in connecting with the divine. They provide structure and meaning to our spiritual lives, helping us focus our intentions and energies. Rituals can be as simple as lighting a candle or as elaborate as a full religious ceremony. Each one honors the sacred and brings us closer to the divine.

One common practice is prayer. Prayer allows individuals to communicate with the divine, expressing their hopes, fears, and gratitude. It can be done silently or aloud, alone or with others. The act of praying helps to center the mind and open the heart to the presence of the divine.

Another important practice is meditation. Meditation involves quieting the mind and turning inward. This practice helps individuals connect with their inner selves and the divine presence. Through meditation, people can experience a sense of peace and clarity that can carry over into their daily lives.

Rituals often involve symbols and actions that represent deeper spiritual truths. For example, lighting a candle can symbolize bringing light into darkness, while offering food can represent gratitude for the abundance of life. These symbolic actions help to make the spiritual more tangible and accessible.

In addition to personal practices, communal rituals can be powerful. Gathering with others to celebrate, pray, or meditate can create a strong sense of connection and shared purpose. These communal experiences remind us that we are part of a larger spiritual community.

MEDITATION AND CONTEMPLATION

Meditation and contemplation are key practices for those seeking a deeper spiritual connection. Both involve quieting the mind and focusing inward, but they have different approaches and goals. Meditation often emphasizes mindfulness and presence, while contemplation is more about reflection and understanding.

Meditation can take many forms. One common practice is focusing on the breath. Individuals can bring their minds into the present moment by paying attention to each inhale and exhale. This helps to reduce stress and increase awareness. Over time, regular meditation can lead to a deeper sense of peace and connection with the divine.

Another form of meditation is the use of mantras. A mantra is a word or phrase repeated during meditation. This repetition helps to focus the mind and keep it from wandering. Mantras can be chosen for their spiritual significance or calming effect. They serve as a tool to deepen one's meditation practice.

Contemplation, on the other hand, involves reflecting on spiritual texts, ideas, or experiences. This practice encourages a deeper understanding of the divine and one's relationship to it. Contemplation often leads to insights and realizations that can transform one's spiritual life. It is a practice of engaging the mind thoughtfully and meaningfully.

Both meditation and contemplation require practice and patience. It's normal for the mind to wander, especially in the beginning. The key is to gently bring the focus back to the chosen point of attention, whether it's the breath, a mantra, or a spiritual idea. Over time, these practices can lead to profound spiritual growth.

PANENTHEISM AND PRAYER

Prayer is a central practice in many spiritual traditions and holds special significance in panentheism. In this view, prayer is a way to communicate with a distant deity and connect with the divine presence within and around us. Prayer becomes a means of aligning ourselves with the sacredness of all life.

One form of prayer in panentheism is gratitude. We acknowledge the divine presence in everyday moments by expressing thanks for the blessings in our lives. Gratitude helps to cultivate a sense of appreciation and connection to the world around us. It reminds us that the divine is present in all aspects of life.

Another form of prayer is intercession, where we ask for help or guidance for ourselves or others. In panentheism, intercessory prayer recognizes that the divine is deeply involved in the world and can influence events and outcomes. This form of prayer reinforces our trust in the divine presence and its ability to bring about positive change.

Contemplative prayer is also important in panentheism. This form of prayer involves quieting the mind and opening the heart to the divine presence. It is less about asking for things and more about simply being in the presence of the sacred. Contemplative prayer fosters a deep sense of peace and connection.

Communal prayer brings people together to honor the divine and support one another. Whether in a formal religious setting or an informal gathering, communal prayer strengthens the bonds between individuals and their spiritual community. It creates a shared space where the divine presence is felt and celebrated.

SPIRITUAL GUIDANCE AND TEACHERS

Spiritual guidance and teachers are crucial in many people's spiritual journeys. They offer wisdom, support, and insights to help individuals navigate their path. In panentheism, spiritual teachers help others recognize the divine presence in all aspects of life and deepen their connection to it.

One of the main roles of a spiritual teacher is to provide guidance. They help individuals understand and apply spiritual principles in their daily lives. This can involve teaching meditation techniques, explaining spiritual texts, or offering practical advice for living a more mindful and connected life.

Mentorship is another important aspect of spiritual guidance. A mentor provides ongoing support and encouragement, helping individuals stay committed to their spiritual practice. This relationship often involves regular meetings, where the mentor listens, offers feedback, and shares their own experiences. This personalized support can be invaluable on the spiritual journey.

Teachers also serve as role models, demonstrating how to live a life that reflects spiritual values. By observing their actions and attitudes, individuals can learn how to embody the principles of panentheism in their own lives. This modeling helps to bridge the gap between theory and practice, making spiritual principles more tangible and accessible.

Community is another key element that spiritual teachers help to foster. By bringing individuals together for group activities and discussions, they create a supportive environment where people can share their experiences and learn from one another. This sense of community helps individuals feel connected and supported on their spiritual path.

Spiritual guidance and teachers provide essential support for those seeking to deepen their connection with the divine. They offer wisdom, mentorship, and community, helping individuals navigate their spiritual journey more clearly and confidently. Through their guidance, people can experience a more profound sense of connection and purpose.

PERSONAL STORIES

Personal stories of spiritual experiences and growth can be powerful sources of inspiration and insight. These narratives provide real-life examples of how individuals have connected with the divine and integrated panentheistic principles into their lives. Sharing these stories helps to build a sense of community and support among those on similar paths.

One common theme in personal stories is the moment of spiritual awakening. Many people describe a specific experience or series of events that opened their eyes to the divine presence in their lives. These moments often involve a deep sense of clarity and understanding, as if a veil has been lifted, revealing the interconnectedness of all things.

Another important aspect of personal stories is the journey of transformation. Individuals often describe how their spiritual experiences have changed them, leading to new perspectives, behaviors, and priorities. These stories highlight the transformative power of connecting with the divine and its positive impact on one's life.

Challenges and struggles are also key to personal stories. Many people face difficulties on their spiritual journey, such as doubt, fear, or resistance. Sharing these struggles helps normalize them and shows that they are a natural part of the process. These stories offer hope and encouragement to others facing similar challenges.

Another common theme is the role of community and support. Many individuals describe how mentors, teachers, and spiritual communities have helped them on their path. These relationships provide guidance, encouragement, and a sense of belonging. Personal stories highlight the importance of seeking and accepting support on the spiritual journey.

Personal stories provide valuable insights into the experiences of those on the spiritual path. They offer inspiration, encouragement, and practical examples of how to integrate panentheistic principles into daily life. By sharing these narratives, individuals can connect with and learn from one another, fostering a sense of community and shared purpose.

INTEGRATION INTO DAILY LIFE

Integrating panentheistic principles into daily life involves making conscious choices that reflect a deep connection with the divine presence in all things. This integration helps bring meaning and purpose to everyday activities, transforming the mundane into the sacred. By living in alignment with these principles, individuals can experience a more connected and fulfilling life.

One way to integrate panentheism into daily life is through mindfulness. By being fully present in each moment, individuals can cultivate a deeper awareness of the divine presence around them. This practice involves paying attention to one's thoughts, feelings, and actions and recognizing the sacredness in everyday experiences.

Another important aspect is gratitude. By regularly expressing thanks for the blessings in our lives, we acknowledge the divine presence in all things. This practice helps to cultivate a positive and appreciative mindset, making it easier to see the interconnectedness and sacredness of life. Gratitude can be expressed through journaling, prayer, or simply taking a moment to reflect.

Acts of service and kindness are also ways to embody panentheistic principles. By helping others and caring for the environment, individuals can honor the divine presence in all beings. These actions reflect a commitment to living in harmony with the interconnectedness of life and contribute to the well-being of the larger community.

Spiritual practices such as meditation, prayer, and ritual can be incorporated into daily routines. These practices provide regular opportunities to connect with the divine presence and reinforce one's spiritual values. By setting aside time each day for these activities, individuals can create a strong foundation for their spiritual lives.

Finally, seeking balance is key to integrating panentheism into daily life. This involves finding harmony between work, rest, and spiritual practice. Individuals can maintain a sense of inner peace and alignment with the divine presence by prioritizing self-care and making time for reflection and connection.

Integrating panentheistic principles into daily life involves conscious choices and practices that reflect a deep connection with the divine. By embracing mindfulness, gratitude, service, and balance, individuals can transform their everyday experiences into opportunities for spiritual growth and connection. This holistic approach helps to create a more meaningful and fulfilling life.

PANENTHEISM AND
PSYCHOLOGY

PSYCHOLOGICAL IMPLICATIONS

P anentheism, the belief that the divine exists in all
things but also transcends them, has profound
psychological implications. It shapes how individuals perceive themselves and their place in the world. By
seeing the divine in all aspects of life, people may develop a
stronger sense of connectedness and purpose. This worldview can foster feelings of unity and belonging, reducing
feelings of isolation.

Understanding the self as part of a larger divine presence can
also impact self-esteem and personal growth. Individuals
may feel more valued and significant, knowing they are part
of something greater. This perspective encourages a holistic
view of self-worth, where personal flaws are seen in the
context of a larger, sacred existence.

Panentheism also influences how people cope with life's
challenges. Believing in a divine presence that permeates all

things can provide comfort and resilience. It offers a sense of support and guidance, helping individuals navigate difficult situations more easily. This belief can reduce anxiety and increase overall well-being.

Furthermore, panentheism can enhance ethical and moral behavior. Seeing the divine in everyone and everything encourages compassionate and respectful interactions. This perspective fosters empathy and altruism, promoting actions that benefit the greater good. It aligns personal behavior with a broader, spiritually grounded ethical framework.

The psychological implications of panentheism are significant. This worldview nurtures a sense of interconnectedness, self-worth, resilience, and ethical behavior. By integrating the divine into all aspects of life, individuals can experience a more fulfilling and balanced psychological state.

JUNGIAN PERSPECTIVES

Carl Jung, a renowned Swiss psychiatrist, introduced concepts that align closely with panentheistic thought. Jung believed in the existence of a collective unconscious, a shared reservoir of experiences and archetypes common to all humanity. This idea resonates with panentheism's emphasis on interconnectedness and the divine presence within all things.

Jung's concept of archetypes, universal symbols, and themes found across cultures reflects the panentheistic view of a shared spiritual reality. These archetypes, such as the hero, the mother, and the shadow, represent fundamental aspects of the human experience. They suggest that deep spiritual truths are embedded within our psyche, connecting us to the divine.

Jung also explored the process of individuation, the journey toward self-realization and wholeness. This process involves integrating different parts of the self, including the conscious and unconscious, to achieve a unified identity. Panentheism supports this journey by emphasizing the divine presence within each individual, guiding them toward greater self-awareness and spiritual growth.

Dream analysis, a key component of Jungian psychology, aligns with panentheistic principles. Jung believed that dreams offer insights into the unconscious mind and the divine. By interpreting dreams, individuals can uncover hidden truths and connect with the deeper spiritual aspects of their existence. This practice encourages a deeper understanding of oneself and the divine.

Jung's emphasis on the integration of opposites, such as light and dark, also resonates with panentheism. This concept suggests that spiritual growth involves embracing all aspects of existence, including the divine and the mundane. It encourages a holistic approach to life, where every experience is seen as an opportunity for spiritual development.

TRANSPERSONAL PSYCHOLOGY

Transpersonal psychology, a field that explores the spiritual aspects of human experience, aligns closely with panentheism. This branch of psychology focuses on the potential for transcendent experiences and the realization of higher states of consciousness. It recognizes the importance of spiritual development in achieving psychological well-being.

One of the core principles of transpersonal psychology is the idea that personal growth involves transcending the ego and connecting with a higher reality. This concept aligns with panentheism's emphasis on the divine presence within all things. By moving beyond self-centered concerns, individuals can experience a deeper connection with the divine and the world around them.

Transpersonal psychology also explores altered states of consciousness, such as those experienced during meditation, prayer, or mystical experiences. These states often reveal the interconnectedness of all life and the presence of the divine. By studying these experiences, transpersonal psychologists aim to understand the spiritual dimensions of human existence.

The concept of self-actualization, popularized by Abraham Maslow, is central to transpersonal psychology. Self-actualization involves realizing one's full potential and achieving a sense of purpose and fulfillment. Panentheism supports this process by emphasizing the divine presence within each individual, guiding them toward their highest potential.

Holotropic breathwork, a technique developed by Stanislav Grof, is another transpersonal practice that aligns with panentheism. This method involves controlled breathing to induce altered states of consciousness and facilitate spiritual healing. Participants often report experiences of unity with the divine and greater self-awareness, reflecting the core principles of panentheism.

MINDFULNESS AND PANENTHEISM

Mindfulness, the practice of being fully present in the moment, has strong connections to panentheistic thought. This practice encourages individuals to observe their thoughts and feelings without judgment, fostering a sense of inner peace and clarity. Mindfulness aligns with panentheism by promoting awareness of the divine presence in every moment.

Practicing mindfulness helps individuals develop a deeper connection with themselves and the world around them. By paying attention to their experiences, people can recognize the interconnectedness of all life. This awareness fosters a sense of unity and harmony, key aspects of panentheistic belief.

Mindfulness also encourages gratitude and appreciation for the present moment. Individuals can cultivate a sense of wonder and reverence for the world by focusing on the here and now. This practice aligns with panentheism's emphasis on seeing the divine in all things, encouraging a more spiritual perspective on daily life.

Incorporating mindfulness into everyday activities can transform mundane tasks into spiritual practices. Whether eating, walking, or working, approaching these activities with mindfulness helps individuals connect with the divine presence. This perspective brings a sense of sacredness to everyday life, reflecting panentheistic principles.

Mindfulness-based stress reduction (MBSR) programs, developed by Jon Kabat-Zinn, demonstrate the practical benefits of this practice. These programs teach mindfulness techniques to help individuals manage stress, pain, and other challenges. By promoting inner peace and resilience, mindfulness supports the psychological well-being that panentheism encourages.

HEALING AND WHOLENESS

The concepts of healing and wholeness are central to both panentheism and psychology. In panentheism, healing involves recognizing and embracing the divine presence within oneself and the world. This perspective encourages individuals to see themselves as part of a larger, sacred whole, fostering a sense of unity and completeness.

Psychological healing often involves addressing and integrating different aspects of the self. The panentheistic view of interconnectedness can enhance this process. Individuals can achieve greater self-acceptance and inner harmony by recognizing the divine presence in all parts of their being. This holistic approach supports mental and emotional well-being.

Therapeutic practices that incorporate panentheistic principles can be particularly effective. For example, integrative therapies that combine traditional psychological techniques with spiritual practices can help individuals achieve deeper healing. These approaches address the mind, body, and spirit, fostering a sense of wholeness and balance.

Spiritual practices such as meditation, prayer, and mindfulness can also play a significant role in healing. These practices help individuals connect with the divine presence, promoting inner peace and resilience. By incorporating these practices into their daily lives, people can support their psychological well-being and spiritual growth.

Community and support are also essential for healing and wholeness. In a panentheistic framework, spiritual communities provide a space for individuals to share their experiences and support one another. These connections foster a sense of belonging and mutual care, enhancing healing.

The concepts of healing and wholeness in panentheism and psychology are deeply interconnected. By recognizing the divine presence within and around us, individuals can achieve greater inner harmony and well-being. This holistic approach supports psychological and spiritual health.

FUTURE RESEARCH

Future research in panentheism and psychology holds great potential. By exploring the intersections of these two areas, researchers can uncover new insights into the nature of human experience and well-being. This research can inform psychological practice and spiritual development, fostering a deeper understanding of the human condition.

One promising area of research is the impact of spiritual practices on mental health. Studies can examine how meditation, prayer, and mindfulness influence psychological well-being. Researchers can develop more effective interventions by identifying the mechanisms through which these practices promote healing.

Another important area of research is the role of community and support in spiritual and psychological health. Investigating how spiritual communities provide social and emotional support can offer insights into the benefits of communal practices. This research can help develop programs that foster a sense of belonging and mutual care.

Integrating traditional psychological therapies with spiritual practices is also a key area for future research. By studying the effectiveness of integrative approaches, researchers can identify best practices for combining these methods. This research can lead to the development of holistic therapeutic models that address the mind, body, and spirit.

Exploring the concept of the collective unconscious and archetypes in modern psychology can also provide valuable insights. Research can examine how these Jungian concepts align with panentheistic principles and their relevance in contemporary therapy. This exploration can deepen our understanding of the interconnectedness of human experience.

Future research in panentheism and psychology has the potential to transform our understanding of well-being. By exploring the intersections of these fields, researchers can uncover new ways to promote healing, growth, and connection. This research can inform both psychological practice and spiritual development, enriching the lives of individuals and communities.

COMPARATIVE THEOLOGY

PANENTHEISM VS. PANTHEISM

Panentheism and pantheism are often confused, but they have distinct differences. Pantheism holds that God and the universe are identical; everything collectively is God. On the other hand, Panentheism posits that while the divine is present in all things, it also extends beyond the universe. This distinction is crucial for understanding their differing views on the nature of the divine.

In pantheism, there is no separation between the creator and the creation. The divine is the sum total of all that exists. This view promotes a strong sense of unity with the natural world, as everything is seen as an expression of the divine. However, it can be criticized for potentially reducing the divine to just the physical universe, lacking a transcendent aspect.

Panentheism maintains a dual aspect of the divine: immanence and transcendence. God is present in every part of the universe but also exists beyond it. This perspective allows for a more dynamic interaction between the divine and the world, suggesting that God influences and is influenced by creation. It provides a more complex and rich understanding of the divine presence.

Both viewpoints encourage a deep respect for nature and the environment. However, panentheism adds an extra layer of reverence by acknowledging a divine presence that permeates and surpasses the physical world. This dual perspective can foster a more profound spiritual connection and a deeper sense of mystery.

Understanding the differences between panentheism and pantheism helps clarify their unique contributions to spiritual thought. While both emphasize the sacredness of the world, panentheism offers a more nuanced view that incorporates both the immanent and transcendent aspects of the divine. This distinction enriches our understanding of the divine and its relationship with the universe.

COMPARISONS WITH DEISM AND THEISM

Deism and theism offer different views of God's relationship with the world, and comparing them with panentheism reveals interesting contrasts. Deism holds that God created the universe but does not interfere with its workings. Theism, particularly in its traditional sense, sees God as both a creator and an active participant in the world. Panentheism combines elements of both, presenting a more integrated view.

Deists believe in a distant, uninvolved creator. This perspective emphasizes the rational structure of the universe, which operates according to natural laws set in motion by God. However, it lacks a sense of ongoing divine presence and interaction. This can make the divine feel remote and impersonal, limiting the sense of spiritual connection.

Theism, especially in monotheistic religions like Christianity, Judaism, and Islam, sees God as actively involved in the world. God listens to prayers, performs miracles, and guides the course of history. This view fosters a personal relationship with the divine but can sometimes create a dualistic separation between God and the world.

Panentheism bridges the gap between deism and theism by emphasizing God's immanence and transcendence. God is not only the creator but also present in every aspect of creation. This view supports a dynamic relationship where the divine is intimately involved in the world yet also beyond it. It encourages a deeper, more personal connection while maintaining a sense of divine mystery.

In practical terms, panentheism offers a more holistic approach to spirituality. It respects the rational order emphasized by deism while embracing the personal involvement seen in theism. This integrated perspective can lead to a richer spiritual experience, balancing faith's logical and emotional aspects.

Comparing panentheism with deism and theism highlights its unique ability to incorporate distance and intimacy in our understanding of the divine. It provides a more comprehensive and balanced view of God's relationship with the world, enhancing our spiritual lives.

DIALOGUES WITH ATHEISM AND AGNOSTICISM

Panentheism also engages in meaningful dialogues with atheism and agnosticism. Atheists deny the existence of God, while agnostics remain uncertain about it. Panentheism, emphasizing the divine presence in all things, offers a unique perspective that can resonate even with those skeptical of traditional religious beliefs.

Atheists often reject the idea of a supernatural deity due to a lack of empirical evidence. Panentheism, however, suggests that the divine can be found within the natural world, in the interconnectedness and complexity of life. This perspective can appeal to those who value scientific understanding and find awe in the mysteries of the universe without needing to believe in a separate, supernatural being.

Agnostics, who claim neither faith nor disbelief in God, often seek a middle ground. Panentheism provides a framework that allows for spiritual exploration without demanding certainty. It invites agnostics to experience the divine in the everyday world, offering a sense of connection and meaning that does not rely on dogmatic beliefs.

Dialogues between panentheists and atheists can be fruitful. They focus on shared values such as awe for the universe, ethical living, and the search for meaning. Both perspectives can agree on the importance of understanding and appreciating the natural world. These conversations can foster mutual respect and open-mindedness, bridging the gap between belief and skepticism.

With agnostics, panentheism can create a space for open exploration. It encourages questioning and seeking, valuing the journey as much as the destination. This approach can help agnostics feel more comfortable engaging with spiritual ideas without feeling pressured to adopt specific doctrines.

Panentheism offers a flexible and inclusive approach that can engage atheists and agnostics in meaningful dialogue. Emphasizing the divine within the natural world and valuing the search for understanding creates common ground for exploring deep questions about existence and meaning.

INTERFAITH PERSPECTIVES

Panentheism has the potential to foster interfaith dialogue and understanding. Emphasizing the divine presence in all things provides common ground for various religious traditions. This perspective can help bridge differences and highlight shared spiritual values, promoting greater harmony among diverse faiths.

Many religions have elements that align with panentheistic thought. For example, Hinduism's concept of Brahman as the ultimate reality that pervades everything resonates with panentheism. Similarly, mystical traditions within Christianity, Judaism, and Islam emphasize the immanence of God, suggesting that the divine is present in all aspects of life.

Panentheism encourages interfaith dialogue by recognizing these commonalities. It helps people see beyond doctrinal differences and appreciate the shared belief in a divine presence that connects all of creation. This understanding can foster mutual respect and cooperation among different religious communities.

Interfaith initiatives often focus on shared ethical values, such as compassion, justice, and stewardship of the Earth. Panentheism supports these efforts by emphasizing the sacredness of all life. It encourages collaborative actions to address global challenges like poverty, environmental degradation, and social injustice, grounded in a shared sense of spiritual responsibility.

Panentheism also promotes a more inclusive and open-minded approach to spirituality. It acknowledges that different religious traditions offer unique insights and practices that can enrich one's spiritual journey. This perspective encourages individuals to learn from and respect each other's beliefs, fostering a more diverse and vibrant spiritual landscape.

PANENTHEISM AND PLURALISM

Panentheism naturally aligns with religious pluralism, the idea that multiple religious traditions can offer valid paths to the divine. By emphasizing the divine presence in all things, panentheism suggests that no single tradition holds a monopoly on spiritual truth. This perspective encourages openness and respect for different spiritual practices and beliefs.

Religious pluralism acknowledges that people have diverse cultural and spiritual backgrounds, leading to various ways of understanding and experiencing the divine. Panentheism supports this diversity by recognizing the divine in all aspects of life, suggesting that each tradition offers unique insights into the sacred. This approach fosters mutual respect and appreciation for different religious paths.

Panentheism also encourages individuals to explore multiple spiritual traditions. It suggests that the divine can be found in many forms and practices, from meditation and prayer to nature walks and artistic expression. This openness allows people to draw from a rich tapestry of spiritual resources, enriching their personal journey.

In a pluralistic society, panentheism can help bridge religious divides. It promotes dialogue and collaboration among different faith communities, emphasizing common values and goals. Focusing on the shared presence of the divine encourages collective action for the greater good, such as environmental stewardship and social justice.

Furthermore, panentheism challenges exclusivist beliefs that claim one religion as the only true path. It promotes a more inclusive understanding of spirituality, where multiple paths lead to the same ultimate reality. This perspective can reduce religious conflict and promote a more harmonious coexistence among diverse faith communities.

Panentheism and pluralism are complementary. They encourage a more inclusive, respectful, and collaborative approach to spirituality. Panentheism supports a rich diversity of religious expressions by recognizing the divine presence in all things, fostering a more connected and compassionate world.

DEBATES AND CRITIQUES

Like any theological perspective, panentheism is debated and critiqued. Some argue that it blurs the line between the creator and creation, potentially leading to confusion about the nature of the divine. Critics worry that emphasizing the divine presence in everything might diminish God's transcendence and otherness.

One common critique is that panentheism could lead to pantheism, where the divine is seen as identical to the universe. This concern arises from the strong focus on the immanence of the divine. Critics argue that this emphasis might overshadow the belief in a transcendent aspect of God, making it difficult to distinguish between the sacred and the secular.

Others question whether panentheism adequately addresses the problem of evil. If the divine is present in all things, how can we explain the existence of suffering and injustice? Critics argue that panentheism must clearly explain how the divine presence interacts with the realities of evil and suffering in the world.

Some traditional theists also critique panentheism for its departure from classical views of God. They argue that it undermines key theological doctrines, such as God's omnipotence and omniscience. By suggesting that the world can influence the divine, panentheism challenges the idea of an all-powerful, unchanging deity.

Despite these critiques, panentheism offers a compelling and holistic view of the divine. Proponents argue that it provides a more integrated understanding of God and the world, fostering a deeper spiritual connection. They suggest that panentheism addresses modern spiritual needs by emphasizing both the immanence and transcendence of the divine.

Debates and critiques of panentheism highlight important theological questions. While it faces challenges, panentheism continues to offer a rich and nuanced perspective on the divine. Engaging in these debates can deepen our understanding and appreciation of this theological view.

FUTURE THEOLOGICAL DIRECTIONS

The future of panentheism holds exciting possibilities for theological exploration and development. As the world becomes more interconnected, panentheism's emphasis on the divine presence in all things can foster a deeper sense of global unity and spiritual connection. This perspective encourages new ways of thinking about spirituality and our relationship with the divine.

One promising direction is the integration of panentheism with scientific understanding. As our knowledge of the universe expands, panentheism can offer a framework for seeing the divine in the complexity and beauty of the natural world. This integration can lead to a richer dialogue between science and spirituality, enhancing both fields.

Environmental theology is another area where panentheism can make significant contributions. Panentheism supports a more profound commitment to environmental stewardship by emphasizing the sacredness of all life. This perspective can inspire new approaches to sustainability and conservation grounded in a deep sense of spiritual responsibility.

Panentheism also has the potential to influence interfaith dialogue and cooperation. Recognizing the divine presence in all religious traditions promotes greater understanding and respect among different faiths. This approach can help build bridges and foster collaboration on shared global challenges.

In addition, panentheism can offer new insights into personal spirituality and mental health. By integrating psychological and spiritual perspectives, panentheism can provide holistic approaches to well-being. This integration can lead to innovative therapies and practices that support mental and emotional health.

The future of panentheism is full of potential for theological growth and innovation. By embracing new ideas and integrating diverse perspectives, panentheism can continue to evolve and inspire. This theological direction holds promise to enrich our spiritual lives and foster a more connected and compassionate world.

CONTEMPORARY ISSUES AND DEBATES

PANENTHEISM AND MODERN SOCIETY

P anentheism, the belief that the divine exists in all things and transcends them, has significant implications for modern society. This worldview can shape how people interact with the world and each other. Panentheism encourages a more compassionate and connected society by seeing the divine presence in all aspects of life.

One of panentheism's key contributions to modern society is its emphasis on the sacredness of nature. In an era of environmental crisis, this perspective fosters a deep respect for the Earth and all its inhabitants. It encourages sustainable practices and a commitment to protecting the natural world, which is seen as an expression of the divine.

Panentheism also promotes a sense of unity and interconnectedness. In a world often divided by cultural, religious, and political differences, this belief can help bridge gaps and foster understanding. Panentheism encourages empathy and cooperation by recognizing the divine in all people, which is essential for addressing global challenges.

Furthermore, panentheism offers a holistic approach to well-being. It integrates physical, mental, and spiritual health, promoting a balanced lifestyle. This perspective can lead to greater personal fulfillment and resilience, helping individuals navigate the complexities of modern life with a sense of purpose and connection.

ETHICAL AND MORAL CHALLENGES

Panentheism brings a unique perspective to ethical and moral challenges. This worldview emphasizes respecting and honoring all life by seeing the divine presence in all things. This perspective can guide individuals and societies in making ethical decisions that reflect a deep sense of responsibility and care.

One of the primary ethical challenges addressed by panentheism is environmental stewardship. Recognizing the divine presence in nature encourages actions that protect and preserve the environment. This perspective supports policies and practices that promote sustainability and reduce harm to the planet, fostering a more harmonious relationship with the Earth.

Social justice is another key area where panentheism can provide ethical guidance. This worldview promotes equality and human rights by seeing the divine in all people. It encourages actions that address systemic injustices and support the well-being of marginalized communities. This perspective fosters a more just and equitable society.

Panentheism also addresses ethical dilemmas related to technology and innovation. As new technologies emerge, they bring both opportunities and challenges. Panentheism encourages the responsible use of technology, ensuring that it benefits humanity and the environment. This perspective supports ethical considerations in the development and application of new technologies.

Personal integrity and ethical behavior are also central to panentheism. Individuals are encouraged to act with honesty, kindness, and respect by recognizing the divine presence within oneself. This perspective fosters a sense of accountability and moral responsibility, guiding individuals in their interactions with others and the world.

TECHNOLOGICAL IMPACTS

The rapid advancement of technology poses significant challenges and opportunities for society. Panentheism offers a valuable perspective on how to navigate these changes responsibly. By emphasizing the divine presence in all things, this worldview encourages the ethical use of technology to enhance human well-being and protect the environment.

One area where technology and panentheism intersect is in environmental sustainability. Technologies that promote renewable energy, reduce waste, and conserve resources align with the panentheistic emphasis on the sacredness of nature. Society can work towards a more sustainable future by adopting and advancing these technologies.

Artificial intelligence (AI) and automation also present ethical considerations. Panentheism encourages the responsible development and use of AI, ensuring that it serves humanity's best interests. This perspective advocates for AI systems that promote fairness, transparency, and respect for human dignity, avoiding harm and bias.

The rise of digital communication and social media has transformed how people interact. Panentheism can guide the ethical use of these platforms by promoting respectful and meaningful connections. It encourages users to recognize the divine presence in others, fostering empathy and reducing harmful behaviors such as cyberbullying and misinformation.

Medical technology and biotechnology also raise important ethical questions. Panentheism supports advancements that enhance human health and well-being while advocating for careful consideration of potential risks and ethical implications. This perspective promotes medical technologies in ways that respect the sanctity of life and the interconnectedness of all beings.

SOCIAL JUSTICE AND PANENTHEISM

Social justice is a core concern of panentheism, which sees the divine presence in all people and emphasizes the interconnectedness of life. This perspective calls for actions that promote equality, human rights, and the well-being of all individuals, particularly those who are marginalized or oppressed.

One of the primary social justice issues addressed by panentheism is economic inequality. Panentheism advocates for fair and equitable distribution of resources by recognizing the divine in everyone. This perspective supports policies and practices that address poverty, ensure access to basic needs, and promote economic opportunities for all.

Racial and ethnic justice is another key area where panentheism provides guidance. This worldview condemns discrimination and promotes the dignity and worth of every individual. It encourages efforts to dismantle systemic racism and support the rights and well-being of all racial and ethnic groups, fostering a more inclusive and equitable society.

Gender equality is also central to the panentheistic view of social justice. By seeing the divine presence in all genders, panentheism advocates for equal rights and opportunities for everyone, regardless of gender. This perspective supports efforts to address gender-based discrimination and violence, promoting a society where all individuals can thrive.

Human rights, in general, are deeply rooted in the panentheistic view of social justice. This perspective calls for the protection and promotion of the rights of all individuals, including the right to education, healthcare, and freedom from oppression. Panentheism supports actions that ensure the well-being and dignity of every person.

Panentheism provides a powerful framework for addressing social justice issues. Its emphasis on the divine presence in all people and the interconnectedness of life inspires actions that promote equality, human rights, and the well-being of all individuals. This perspective can guide efforts to create a more just and compassionate society.

GLOBALIZATION AND INTERCONNECTIVITY

Globalization has brought about unprecedented levels of interconnectivity, linking people, cultures, and economies worldwide. Panentheism, with its emphasis on the divine presence in all things and the interconnectedness of life, offers a valuable perspective for navigating the complexities of globalization.

One key benefit of globalization is the increased exchange of ideas and cultures. Panentheism encourages an appreciation for the diversity of human experience, recognizing the divine presence in all cultures and traditions. This perspective fosters respect and understanding, promoting cross-cultural dialogue and cooperation.

However, globalization also presents challenges like economic disparities and cultural homogenization. Panentheism advocates addressing these issues by promoting equitable economic policies and preserving cultural diversity. By recognizing the divine in all people, this perspective supports actions that ensure fair opportunities and respect for all cultures.

Environmental sustainability is another critical issue in the context of globalization. The interconnected nature of global ecosystems means that actions in one part of the world can impact the entire planet. Panentheism emphasizes the sacredness of the Earth and the need for collective action to protect it. This perspective supports international cooperation on environmental issues.

Globalization also impacts social justice, as global economic systems can exacerbate inequalities. Panentheism calls for actions that address these disparities, ensuring that the benefits of globalization are shared equitably. This perspective promotes policies that protect vulnerable populations and support sustainable development.

POLITICAL IMPLICATIONS

Panentheism, with its view of the divine presence in all things, has significant political implications. This perspective can shape policies and actions reflecting a deep sense of responsibility and care for everyone and the planet. Societies can work towards more just and compassionate governance by integrating panentheistic principles into political decision-making.

One of panentheism's key political implications is the promotion of environmental policies. Panentheism advocates for laws and regulations that protect the environment, recognizing the sacredness of nature. This perspective supports initiatives to address climate change, conserve natural resources, and promote sustainable development.

Social justice is another area where panentheism can influence politics. By seeing the divine in all people, this worldview supports policies that promote equality and human rights. It encourages actions to address systemic injustices, such as poverty, discrimination, and healthcare disparities, fostering a more equitable society.

Panentheism also emphasizes the importance of community and interconnectedness. This perspective can guide political efforts to strengthen social bonds and support community development. Policies that promote education, public health, and social services align with panentheistic principles, ensuring the well-being of all citizens.

Economic policies are also shaped by panentheistic values. By advocating for fair and equitable distribution of resources, panentheism supports policies that address economic inequality. This perspective encourages measures to ensure that everyone has access to basic needs and opportunities for economic advancement.

The political implications of panentheism are far-reaching. By integrating this worldview into governance, societies can develop policies that reflect a deep respect for the environment, promote social justice, strengthen communities, and address economic disparities. Panentheism offers a holistic political approach that fosters a more compassionate and sustainable world.

FUTURE PROSPECTS

The future prospects of panentheism are promising, as this worldview offers valuable insights for addressing contemporary challenges. As societies grapple with issues such as environmental degradation, social injustice, and technological advancements, panentheism provides a framework for integrating spiritual principles into practical solutions.

One area of future development is the integration of panentheism with scientific research. Panentheism can contribute to a deeper understanding of the natural world by fostering dialogue between spirituality and science. This integration can lead to innovative approaches to environmental conservation, health, and technology grounded in a sense of spiritual responsibility.

Panentheism also has the potential to influence education. By incorporating panentheistic principles into curricula, educators can promote a holistic understanding of interconnectedness and the sacredness of life. This approach can inspire students to develop a deeper appreciation for the environment and commit to social justice.

Panentheism can continue to play a vital role in interfaith dialogue. Panentheism supports efforts to foster mutual respect and cooperation among diverse faith communities by emphasizing the divine presence in all religious traditions. This perspective can help build bridges and promote peace in an increasingly interconnected world.

The future of panentheism also includes the development of new spiritual practices and communities. As more people seek meaningful connections and holistic well-being, panentheism can provide a rich and inclusive framework for spiritual growth. This perspective encourages the exploration of diverse spiritual traditions and the creation of supportive communities.

The future prospects of panentheism are bright. By integrating this worldview into various aspects of society, we can address contemporary challenges with a sense of interconnectedness and spiritual responsibility. Panentheism offers a promising path to create a more compassionate, sustainable, and connected world.

PANENTHEISM IN
CONTEMPORARY CULTURE

PANENTHEISM IN LITERATURE

Panentheism has profoundly impacted literature, with many authors exploring its themes through their works. Writers often explore the idea of the divine being present in all things, weaving this concept into their narratives to create a sense of interconnectedness. This theme can be seen in both classic and contemporary literature, where characters and settings are infused with a sense of the sacred. Through this literary lens, readers are invited to view the world as a place where the divine and the mundane coexist seamlessly.

In novels, panentheistic ideas often manifest in how characters interact with nature. A common trope is the portrayal of landscapes as living, breathing entities imbued with spiritual significance. Authors use this to highlight the unity between humanity and the environment, suggesting that everything is interconnected. This approach enriches the narrative and encourages readers to reflect on their relationship with the natural world.

Poetry is another genre where panentheism thrives. Poets use rich, evocative language to express the presence of the divine in everyday experiences. Their verses capture moments of transcendence that occur in ordinary settings, making the mundane seem miraculous. This poetic expression of panentheism helps readers to see the beauty and sacredness in their daily lives, fostering a deeper appreciation for the world around them.

Short stories also explore panentheistic themes, often through allegory and metaphor. These concise narratives can powerfully convey the interconnectedness of all things, using symbolism to illustrate the presence of the divine in the world. Doing so offers readers a glimpse into a worldview where everything is part of a greater whole, encouraging contemplation and introspection.

In children's literature, panentheism is subtly introduced to young readers through stories emphasizing harmony with nature and the interconnectedness of life. These stories often feature animals, plants, and natural elements as characters, teaching children about the sacredness of all living things. This early exposure to panentheistic ideas helps to instill a sense of wonder and respect for the world, laying the foundation for a lifelong appreciation of the interconnectedness of life.

REPRESENTATION IN FILM AND MEDIA

Film and media have also embraced panentheistic themes, using visual storytelling to convey the presence of the divine in all aspects of life. Movies often explore these ideas through cinematography, creating scenes that highlight the beauty and interconnectedness of the natural world. Directors use light, color, and composition to evoke a sense of the sacred, making the audience feel as if they are witnessing something profound.

Documentaries, in particular, have been instrumental in showcasing panentheistic ideas. Films about nature and the environment often emphasize the interconnectedness of ecosystems, portraying the natural world as a complex, interdependent web of life. These documentaries educate viewers about ecological issues and inspire a sense of awe and reverence for the planet. They convey that everything is connected and sacred through stunning visuals and compelling narratives.

Television series have also explored panentheistic themes, especially in science fiction and fantasy genres. These shows often feature worlds where the boundaries between the divine and the mundane are blurred, and characters interact with forces greater than themselves. By presenting these themes in an entertaining format, television can reach a wide audience and introduce complex philosophical ideas in an accessible way.

Animation has been a powerful medium for expressing panentheism with its limitless creative possibilities. Animated films and series often use imaginative visuals to depict the divine presence in nature and everyday life. Through vibrant colors and fantastical settings, animators can create a sense of wonder and magic, making the idea of interconnectedness tangible and engaging for viewers of all ages.

The influence of panentheism in video games is also notable. Many games create immersive worlds where players can experience the interconnectedness of all things firsthand. Game designers use rich, detailed environments to convey the presence of the divine, encouraging players to explore and appreciate the unity of the game world. This interactive medium allows for a unique exploration of panentheistic ideas, making them accessible and engaging in a way that is both entertaining and thought-provoking.

INFLUENCE ON MODERN ART

Modern art has been deeply influenced by panentheistic ideas, with many artists exploring the theme of interconnectedness in their work. Abstract and conceptual art, in particular, often examine the relationship between the divine and the mundane. Artists use color, form, and texture to create pieces that evoke a sense of unity and transcendence, inviting viewers to experience the sacred in new and unexpected ways.

Installation art provides a unique platform for expressing panentheism. By creating immersive environments, artists can envelop viewers in a space that feels both ordinary and extraordinary. These installations often incorporate natural elements, light, and sound to evoke a sense of the divine presence. As viewers move through the space, they experience the interconnectedness of all things, making panentheism tangible and visceral.

Public art and murals also play a significant role in bringing panentheistic ideas to the broader community. By integrating art into public spaces, artists can transform everyday environments into places of reflection and connection.

Murals that depict scenes of nature, community, and spirituality help to remind viewers of the sacredness of their surroundings, fostering a sense of unity and interconnectedness within the community.

Photography has also been a powerful medium for exploring panentheism. Photographers capture moments of transcendence in the natural world and urban landscapes, highlighting the beauty and sacredness in the mundane. Through their lenses, they reveal the interconnectedness of all things, encouraging viewers to see the divine in their everyday lives. This visual representation of panentheism helps to bridge the gap between the abstract concept and the tangible world.

Digital art and new media have opened up even more possibilities for expressing panentheistic themes. Artists use technology to create interactive and multimedia pieces that explore the relationship between the divine and the everyday. These works often incorporate elements like virtual reality and augmented reality to create immersive experiences that engage viewers on multiple sensory levels. By leveraging the capabilities of new media, artists can convey the interconnectedness of all things in innovative and compelling ways.

PANENTHEISM AND MUSIC

Music has always been a powerful medium for expressing spiritual ideas; panentheism is no exception. Composers and musicians often draw on the theme of interconnectedness in their work, creating pieces that evoke a sense of unity and transcendence. They capture the divine presence in the world through melody, harmony, and rhythm, offering listeners an auditory experience of panentheism.

Classical music, with its rich history of spiritual and religious themes, has many examples of panentheistic influence. Composers like Beethoven and Mahler created symphonies that explore the relationship between the divine and the human. Their music often conveys a sense of awe and reverence for the natural world, reflecting the idea that everything is interconnected and imbued with the sacred.

Modern and contemporary music genres also explore panentheistic themes. Ambient and electronic music, for example, often uses soundscapes to create an immersive listening experience that evokes the interconnectedness of all things. These genres blend natural sounds with electronic elements to create a sense of unity between the organic and the technological, reflecting the panentheistic idea that the divine is present in all aspects of life.

Folk and world music traditions have long incorporated panentheistic themes, often drawing on indigenous and cultural beliefs about the sacredness of nature. These musical traditions use instruments, rhythms, and melodies that evoke a deep connection to the earth and the cosmos. By preserving and sharing these traditions, musicians help to keep the panentheistic worldview alive and relevant in contemporary society.

In popular music, artists often explore unity, transcendence, and interconnectedness themes in their lyrics and compositions. Songs that celebrate the beauty of nature, the power of love, and the wonder of existence resonate with panentheistic ideas. Popular music can introduce and reinforce these themes by reaching a wide audience, making them accessible and relatable to listeners of all backgrounds.

Live music performances and festivals provide opportunities for communal experiences of panentheism. Concerts and gatherings that focus on themes of unity and connection create a shared space where attendees can feel a sense of belonging and transcendence. These events often emphasize the interconnectedness of all participants, fostering a sense of community and reinforcing the idea that the divine is present in all aspects of life.

IMPACT ON EDUCATION AND ACADEMIA

Panentheism has made significant inroads into education and academia, influencing teaching and research. In philosophy and theology departments, scholars explore the implications of panentheism for understanding the nature of reality and the divine. These academic pursuits help to deepen and expand the philosophical and theological foundations of panentheism, making it a subject of serious study and debate.

Panentheism provides a framework for understanding the interconnectedness of all life in environmental studies and ecology programs. Educators use panentheistic principles to teach students about the importance of sustainability and stewardship. By framing environmental issues regarding sacred interconnectedness, they encourage a sense of responsibility and reverence for the natural world.

Panentheism also influences education in the arts and humanities. Literature, music, and art history courses often explore how panentheistic themes have shaped creative expression. By examining these influences, students gain a deeper appreciation for the interconnectedness of culture, spirituality, and the natural world. This interdisciplinary approach enriches their understanding and broadens their intellectual horizons.

In education policy and pedagogy, panentheistic ideas can inspire more holistic and inclusive approaches to teaching. Educators who embrace these principles often emphasize the importance of community, collaboration, and the development of the whole person. By fostering a sense of interconnectedness and shared responsibility, they create learning environments that are supportive, inclusive, and nurturing.

Academic research on panentheism continues to grow, with scholars from diverse fields contributing to the discourse. This research explores panentheism's philosophical, theological, and practical implications, shedding light on its relevance to contemporary issues. By advancing knowledge in this area, academia helps to ensure that panentheism remains a vibrant and dynamic field of study.

PANENTHEISM IN POPULAR CULTURE

Panentheism has also found its way into popular culture, influencing everything from fashion to social media. The themes of interconnectedness and unity resonate with many people, making panentheistic ideas accessible and appealing. By integrating these concepts into everyday life, popular culture helps to spread awareness and understanding of panentheism.

Fashion designers often draw on panentheistic themes in their work, creating collections that emphasize the beauty and interconnectedness of nature. Using sustainable materials and eco-friendly practices they promote a sense of responsibility and reverence for the environment. These designs make a fashion statement and convey a deeper message about the importance of living in harmony with the world around us.

Social media platforms allow individuals to share and explore panentheistic ideas. Influencers and content creators often use their platforms to promote themes of unity, interconnectedness, and mindfulness. By sharing inspirational quotes, nature photography, and personal reflections, they help to foster a sense of community and connection among their followers.

Television shows and movies also incorporate panentheistic themes, often through storylines that explore the relationship between humans and the natural world. Characters who find meaning and purpose through their connection to nature reflect the panentheistic belief that the divine is present in all things. These narratives resonate with audiences, offering a sense of hope and inspiration.

In wellness and self-care, panentheistic principles are often integrated into practices like yoga, meditation, and mindfulness. These activities emphasize the interconnectedness of mind, body, and spirit, encouraging individuals to cultivate a sense of inner peace and harmony. Promoting these practices helps the wellness industry make panentheistic ideas more accessible and relevant to everyday life.

The popularity of environmental activism and sustainability movements also reflects the influence of panentheistic ideas. Activists who emphasize the sacredness of the earth and the interconnectedness of all life draw on panentheistic principles to inspire change. By advocating for policies and practices that protect the environment, they help to promote a sense of responsibility and reverence for the natural world.

FUTURE CULTURAL TRENDS

Looking to the future, panentheism is likely to continue to influence cultural trends in various ways. As society becomes more aware of the interconnectedness of all things, the principles of panentheism will resonate more deeply. This awareness will likely manifest in an increased emphasis on sustainability, community, and holistic approaches to life.

One potential trend is the integration of panentheistic ideas into technology and innovation. As technology advances, there may be more emphasis on creating solutions that reflect the interconnectedness of all things. This could lead to more sustainable and eco-friendly technologies that promote harmony with the environment.

In the arts, we may see a continued exploration of panentheistic themes, with artists using new mediums and techniques to convey the interconnectedness of life. Virtual reality and augmented reality could provide new ways for people to experience the divine presence in the world, creating immersive experiences that highlight the unity of all things.

Education will likely continue to incorporate panentheistic principles, with an emphasis on holistic and interdisciplinary approaches. As educators recognize the importance of interconnectedness, they will create curricula that reflect these values, fostering a sense of responsibility and reverence for the world among students.

In popular culture, panentheistic ideas will likely become even more mainstream. As people seek meaning and connection in their lives, the themes of unity and interconnectedness will resonate more deeply. This could lead to more widespread adoption of practices like mindfulness, meditation, and sustainable living.

The future of panentheism in contemporary culture looks bright. As society continues to evolve, the principles of interconnectedness and unity will likely play an increasingly important role. By embracing these ideas, we can create a more harmonious and sustainable world for future generations.

AFTERWORD

SUMMARY OF KEY POINTS

Throughout this book, we have explored the fascinating concept of panentheism and its profound implications. We began by defining panentheism, distinguishing it from related theological views, and tracing its historical roots. By examining its core principles, we delved into the belief that the divine is both immanent and transcendent, permeating every part of the universe while also existing beyond it. This dual aspect of the divine forms the foundation of panentheism, creating a unique perspective on spirituality and existence.

We then examined how panentheism compares to other theological and philosophical systems. By contrasting it with pantheism, theism, deism, and process theology, we highlighted its distinctive features. This comparison helped clarify panentheism's unique position in the broader landscape of religious and philosophical thought. Understanding these differences is crucial for appreciating the nuances and depth of panentheistic beliefs.

Historical and contemporary thinkers who have contributed to the development of panentheism were also discussed. Figures like Plato, Spinoza, Whitehead, and Tillich have all played significant roles in shaping panentheistic ideas. By examining their contributions, we gained insights into how panentheism has evolved and continues to influence modern thought. These thinkers provide a rich intellectual heritage that underpins contemporary panentheistic discussions.

Another key point was the application of panentheism in various religious traditions. We explored how panentheistic ideas manifest in Christianity, Eastern religions, and indigenous beliefs. Each tradition brings its unique perspective to panentheism, enriching our understanding of how the divine and the world are interconnected. This exploration showed that panentheism is not confined to any single religion but is a concept that transcends cultural and theological boundaries.

Finally, we examined the impact of panentheism on contemporary culture. From literature and film to art and music, panentheistic themes are prevalent in many forms of creative expression. These cultural manifestations reflect the ongoing relevance of panentheism and its ability to inspire and resonate with people today. By recognizing these influences, we can see how panentheism continues to shape and be shaped by the world around us.

PERSONAL REFLECTIONS

As we come to the end of this journey, it's worth taking a moment to reflect on the personal impact of panentheism. For many, the idea that the divine is present in all things brings a profound sense of connection and meaning. It challenges us to see the sacred in the mundane to recognize the beauty and divinity in everyday life. This perspective can transform our relationship with the world, making us more mindful and appreciative of the interconnectedness of all things.

Panentheism also invites us to reconsider our place in the universe. It suggests that we are not separate from the divine but are part of a larger, interconnected whole. This can be both humbling and empowering. It encourages us to act with greater compassion and responsibility, knowing that our actions impact the entire web of existence. This sense of interconnectedness can inspire us to live more ethically and sustainably, recognizing our role in the larger tapestry of life.

On a personal level, panentheism can also provide comfort and solace. In times of difficulty or uncertainty, believing that the divine is present in all things can offer peace and reassurance. It reminds us that we are never truly alone, that we are part of a larger, divine reality. This can be a source of strength and resilience, helping us navigate life's challenges with a greater sense of purpose and hope.

Reflecting on the ideas presented in this book, it becomes clear that panentheism is not just a theological concept but a way of life. It encourages us to see the world through a lens of wonder and reverence to appreciate the sacredness of all things. By embracing this perspective, we can cultivate a deeper connection to ourselves, others, and the world around us.

Ultimately, the journey through panentheism is a deeply personal one. Each individual's experience will be unique, shaped by their own beliefs, experiences, and reflections. As we conclude this exploration, I encourage you to continue reflecting on these ideas to consider how they resonate with your life and beliefs. Panentheism offers a rich and rewarding path for those who seek a deeper understanding of the divine and our place in the universe.

THE FUTURE OF PANENTHEISM

Looking ahead, the future of panentheism appears bright and full of potential. As society continues to evolve, the principles of interconnectedness and unity that underpin panentheism are becoming increasingly relevant. The panentheistic perspective offers a valuable framework for addressing these issues in a world faced with environmental challenges, social divisions, and technological advancements.

One area where panentheism is likely to have a significant impact is environmental sustainability. As awareness of the interconnectedness of all life grows, more people are recognizing the importance of living in harmony with the natural world. Panentheism's emphasis on the sacredness of all things can inspire more sustainable practices and policies, fostering a greater sense of responsibility towards the environment. This perspective can help to drive meaningful change, promoting a more balanced and respectful relationship with the planet.

In science and technology, panentheism also has the potential to inspire new ways of thinking. As scientific understanding deepens, the physical and spiritual boundaries are becoming increasingly blurred. Panentheism's holistic approach can encourage scientists and technologists to explore the interconnectedness of all things, leading to innovations more aligned with the principles of unity and sustainability. This can result in advancements that enhance our understanding of the universe and promote the well-being of all life.

Culturally, panentheism is likely to continue influencing art, literature, and media. As creators seek to explore themes of interconnectedness and transcendence, panentheistic ideas will continue to find expression in various forms of artistic and literary work. This ongoing cultural engagement can help to keep panentheism relevant and accessible, reaching new audiences and inspiring fresh perspectives.

Education is another area where panentheism can play a crucial role. By integrating panentheistic principles into curricula, educators can foster a greater sense of interconnectedness and responsibility in students. This can help cultivate a new generation of thinkers and leaders who are mindful of the sacredness of all life and committed to creating a more just and sustainable world.

Ultimately, the future of panentheism will be shaped by those who embrace its principles and apply them in their lives. As more people come to appreciate the interconnectedness of all things, panentheism can serve as a guiding light, offering a path towards a more compassionate, sustainable, and harmonious world. By fostering a deeper understanding of our relationship with the divine and the universe, panentheism can potentially transform not only individual lives but society as a whole.

PANENTHEISM IN DAILY LIFE

Panentheism is not just a concept to be studied but a way of life that can be integrated into our daily routines. Embracing the idea that the divine is present in all things can fundamentally change how we perceive and interact with the world. This perspective encourages us to live with greater mindfulness, compassion, and reverence, transforming ordinary moments into opportunities for connection and transcendence.

One way to incorporate panentheism into daily life is through mindfulness practices. By taking time each day to be present and aware, we can cultivate a deeper appreciation for the interconnectedness of all things. Whether through meditation, prayer, or simply spending time in nature, these practices help us to connect with the divine presence that permeates everything. This can lead to a greater sense of peace and fulfillment as we become more attuned to the sacredness of our surroundings.

Acts of kindness and compassion are another way to live out panentheistic principles. Recognizing the divine in others encourages us to treat them with respect and empathy. By extending kindness to those around us, we honor the interconnectedness of all life and contribute to a more compassionate and just world. Simple gestures of generosity and support can profoundly impact and foster a sense of unity and community.

Sustainable living is also a natural extension of panentheistic beliefs. By making choices that are mindful of the environment, we acknowledge the sacredness of the natural world and our responsibility to care for it. This can involve reducing waste, conserving resources, and supporting eco-friendly practices and products. Living sustainably benefits the planet and reinforces our connection to the divine presence in all things.

Personal reflection and journaling can also be valuable tools for integrating panentheism into daily life. Reflecting on our experiences and how we encounter the divine can deepen our understanding and appreciation of panentheistic principles. Writing about these reflections helps to solidify our insights and keep us mindful of the interconnectedness of all things. This practice can be both grounding and inspiring, providing a sense of clarity and purpose.

Finally, cultivating a sense of wonder and gratitude is essential for living a panentheistic life. By approaching each day with curiosity and appreciation, we open ourselves to the beauty and sacredness of the world around us. Whether through marveling at a sunset, appreciating the complexity of a flower, or feeling gratitude for the people in our lives, these moments of wonder and thankfulness help to keep us connected to the divine presence that infuses everything.

FURTHER READING AND RESOURCES

There are many excellent resources available for those interested in delving deeper into the concepts and implications of panentheism. Books, articles, and online materials offer a wealth of information on panentheism's history, philosophy, and practice. These resources can provide a deeper understanding of the principles discussed in this book and offer new perspectives on the interconnectedness of all things.

Readers can explore the works of key thinkers who have shaped panentheistic thought, starting with foundational texts. Philosophical writings by figures like Alfred North Whitehead and Charles Hartshorne provide a deep dive into the metaphysical aspects of panentheism. Their works offer detailed explorations of how the divine interacts with the world, providing a solid intellectual foundation for understanding panentheistic principles.

Theological works by contemporary scholars also offer valuable insights. Books by authors such as John Cobb, David Ray Griffin, and Philip Clayton explore the theological implications of panentheism in the context of modern religious thought. These works often bridge the gap between philosophy and practical theology, making them accessible to readers from diverse backgrounds.

Numerous resources explore the dynamic relationship between panentheism and science. Books and articles on topics like process theology, the relationship between science and religion, and the role of consciousness in the universe provide fascinating insights. These resources help illustrate how panentheistic principles can inform and be informed by scientific understanding.

In addition to scholarly works, there are many accessible books and articles written for a general audience. These resources often focus on the practical applications of panentheism, offering guidance on how to integrate its principles into daily life. They may include personal reflections, practical exercises, and inspiring stories that make panentheism relevant and engaging for everyday readers.

Online resources, including websites, blogs, and online courses, also offer valuable opportunities for exploration. Many organizations and institutions dedicated to panentheism provide information and support for those interested in learning more. These resources can be particularly helpful for connecting with a community of like-minded individuals and staying up-to-date with the latest developments in the field.

ENCOURAGEMENT FOR EXPLORATION

As we conclude this book, I encourage you to continue exploring the rich and rewarding world of panentheism. This journey of discovery does not end here but is an ongoing process of learning, reflection, and growth. By remaining curious and open-minded, you can deepen your understanding of panentheism and its implications for your life and the world around you.

Exploration can take many forms. You might choose to read more about panentheism, exploring the works of scholars and thinkers who have contributed to this field. Engaging with different perspectives can help expand your understanding and challenge your assumptions, leading to new insights and a deeper appreciation for the interconnectedness of all things.

Practical exploration is equally important. Consider integrating panentheistic principles into your daily life through mindfulness practices, acts of kindness, or sustainable living. These actions help to embody the principles of panentheism, making them a tangible part of your everyday experience. Living out these values contributes to a more compassionate and harmonious world.

Engaging with others interested in panentheism can also be incredibly enriching. Joining discussion groups, attending lectures or workshops, and participating in online forums can provide opportunities to share ideas, ask questions, and learn from others. Building connections with like-minded individuals fosters a sense of community and support, enhancing your exploration of panentheism.

Creative exploration is another powerful way to engage with panentheism. Whether through writing, art, music, or other forms of expression, you can explore and communicate your understanding of the divine and its presence in the world. Creativity allows for a unique and personal exploration of panentheistic themes, providing new ways to connect with and express the sacredness of all things.

Ultimately, the journey of exploration is deeply personal and unique to each individual. There is no single path to understanding and experiencing panentheism; each person's journey will be shaped by their own experiences, interests, and reflections. By remaining open and curious, you can continue to discover how panentheism enriches your understanding of the divine and the world.

FINAL THOUGHTS

As we reach the end of this book, it is clear that panentheism offers a profound and transformative perspective on the divine and our place in the universe. By embracing the idea that the divine is present in all things, we can cultivate a deeper sense of connection, meaning, and purpose in our lives. This perspective challenges us to see the world through new eyes, recognizing the sacredness and interconnectedness of all things.

Panentheism invites us to live with greater mindfulness and compassion to appreciate the beauty and divinity in everyday life. It encourages us to act with responsibility and reverence, recognizing our impact on the world and our role in the larger web of existence. By embodying these principles, we can create a more harmonious and sustainable world for ourselves and future generations.

The journey through panentheism is ongoing, offering endless opportunities for exploration and growth. Each person's path will be unique, shaped by their own experiences and reflections. By remaining curious and open-minded, we can continue to deepen our understanding of panentheism and its implications for our lives and the world around us.

I hope this book has provided valuable insights and inspiration for your journey. Whether you are new to panentheism or have been exploring its principles for some time, there is always more to discover and learn. By embracing the interconnectedness of all things, we can cultivate a deeper sense of wonder, gratitude, and reverence for the world.

Thank you for joining me on this journey through panentheism. May your exploration be rich and rewarding, and may you find inspiration and meaning in the sacredness of all things. As you continue to reflect on and engage with these ideas, I hope you find new ways to connect with the divine and enrich your understanding of the interconnectedness of life.

GLOSSARY

Abstract - Existing in thought or as an idea but not having a physical or concrete existence.

Allegory - A story, poem, or picture that can be interpreted to reveal a hidden meaning.

Ambient - Relating to the immediate surroundings of something.

Asceticism - Severe self-discipline and avoidance of all forms of indulgence.

Awe - A feeling of reverential respect mixed with fear or wonder.

Compassion - Sympathetic pity and concern for the sufferings or misfortunes of others.

Cosmology - The science of the origin and development of the universe.

Deism - Belief in the existence of a supreme being, specifically of a creator who does not intervene in the universe.

Divine - Of, from, or like God or a god.

Ecumenical - Representing a number of different Christian churches.

Empathy - The ability to understand and share the feelings of another.

Enlightenment - The action of enlightening or the state of being enlightened.

Epistemology - The theory of knowledge, especially with regard to its methods, validity, and scope.

Ethics - Moral principles that govern a person's behavior.

Evolution - The gradual development of something, especially from a simple to a more complex form.

Existence - The fact or state of living or having objective reality.

Harmony - The combination of simultaneously sounded musical notes to produce chords and chord progressions.

Holistic - Characterized by comprehension of the parts of something as intimately interconnected.

Immanence - Existing or operating within; inherent.

Indigenous - Originating or occurring naturally in a particular place; native.

Interconnectedness - The state of being connected with each other.

Jainism - An ancient religion from India that teaches the way to liberation and bliss is to live a life of harmlessness and renunciation.

Metaphysics - The branch of philosophy that deals with the first principles of things.

Mindfulness - The quality or state of being conscious or aware of something.

Monotheism - The doctrine or belief that there is only one God.

Mysticism - Belief that union with or absorption into the Deity or the absolute can be attained through contemplation and self-surrender.

Ontology - The branch of metaphysics dealing with the nature of being.

Pantheism - The belief that the universe and nature are equivalent to God.

Philosophy - The study of the fundamental nature of knowledge, reality, and existence.

Poetry - Literary work in which the expression of feelings and ideas is given intensity by the use of distinctive style and rhythm.

Process Theology - A type of theology influenced by the process philosophy of Alfred North Whitehead.

Reformation - The action or process of reforming an institution or practice.

Renaissance - The revival of art and literature under the influence of classical models in the 14th–16th centuries.

Sacred - Connected with God or dedicated to a religious purpose and so deserving veneration.

Shamanism - A religion practiced by indigenous peoples of far northern Europe and Siberia, characterized by belief in an unseen world of gods, demons, and ancestral spirits.

Sustainability - The ability to be maintained at a certain rate or level.

Symbiosis - Interaction between two different organisms living in close physical association.

Syncretism - The amalgamation or attempted amalgamation of different religions, cultures, or schools of thought.

Taoism - A Chinese philosophy based on the writings of Lao-tzu advocating humility and religious piety.

Theism - Belief in the existence of a god or gods.

Transcendence - Existence or experience beyond the normal or physical level.

Unity - The state of being united or joined as a whole.

Universe - All existing matter and space considered as a whole.

Virtual Reality - The computer-generated simulation of a three-dimensional image or environment.

Wonder - A feeling of amazement and admiration, caused by something beautiful, remarkable, or unfamiliar.

Yoga - A Hindu spiritual and ascetic discipline, including breath control, simple meditation, and the adoption of specific bodily postures.

Zen - A Japanese school of Mahayana Buddhism emphasizing the value of meditation and intuition.

SUGGESTED READINGS

David Ray Griffin - *Reenchantment Without Supernaturalism: A Process Philosophy of Religion*

Philip Clayton - *Adventures in the Spirit: God, World, Divine Action*

John B. Cobb Jr. - *A Christian Natural Theology: Based on the Thought of Alfred North Whitehead*

John B. Cobb Jr. and **David Ray Griffin** - *Process Theology: An Introductory Exposition*

Matthew Fox - *Creation Spirituality: Liberating Gifts for the Peoples of the Earth*

Michael E. Lodahl - *The Story of God: A Narrative Theology*

Niels Henrik Gregersen - *Incarnation: On the Scope and Depth of Christology*

Sallie McFague - *Models of God: Theology for an Ecological, Nuclear Age*

Sallie McFague - *The Body of God: An Ecological Theology*

Catherine Keller - *Face of the Deep: A Theology of Becoming*

Catherine Keller - *Cloud of the Impossible: Negative Theology and Planetary Entanglement*

Thomas Jay Oord - *The Uncontrolling Love of God: An Open and Relational Account of Providence*

Thomas Jay Oord - *God Can't: How to Believe in God and Love after Tragedy, Abuse, and Other Evils*

Alfred North Whitehead - *Process and Reality*

Philip Hefner - *The Human Factor: Evolution, Culture, and Religion*

Douglas F. Ottati - *God and the Moral Life*

Arthur Peacocke - *Theology for a Scientific Age: Being and Becoming - Natural, Divine and Human*

Jay McDaniel - *With Roots & Wings: Christianity in an Age of Ecology and Dialogue*

David Bohm - *Wholeness and the Implicate Order*

Ian Barbour - *Religion and Science: Historical and Contemporary Issues*

Printed in Great Britain
by Amazon

42684173R10089